Applying Color Theory to

Digital Media
and
Visualization

Applying Color Theory to
Digital Media
and
Visualization

Theresa-Marie Rhyne
Visualization Consultant
Durham, North Carolina, USA

CRC Press
Taylor & Francis Group
Boca Raton   London   New York

CRC Press is an imprint of the
Taylor & Francis Group, an **informa** business

CRC Press
Taylor & Francis Group
6000 Broken Sound Parkway NW, Suite 300
Boca Raton, FL 33487-2742

First issued in hardback 2017

ISBN 13: 978-1-138-41354-2 (hbk)
ISBN 13: 978-1-4987-6549-7 (pbk)

Library of Congress Cataloging-in-Publication Data

Names: Rhyne, Theresa-Marie, author.
Title: Applying color theory to digital media and visualization /
Theresa-Marie Rhyne.
Description: Boca Raton : Taylor & Francis, a CRC title, part of the Taylor &
Francis imprint, a member of the Taylor & Francis Group, the academic
division of T&F Informa, plc, [2017] | Includes bibliographical references
and index.
Identifiers: LCCN 2016018402 | ISBN 9781498765497 (alk. paper)
Subjects: LCSH: Color--Data processing. | Color in design. | Color computer
graphics. | Color vision. | Information visualization.
Classification: LCC QC495.8 .R58 2017 | DDC 006.601--dc23
LC record available at https://lccn.loc.gov/2016018402

Visit the Taylor & Francis Web site at
http://www.taylorandfrancis.com

and the CRC Press Web site at
http://www.crcpress.com

With much love to my parents, Marie Britt Rhyne, MD, and Jimmie Lee Rhyne, MD, for knowing in their hearts that I would one day write this book.

Contents

Acknowledgments

I T HAS BEEN A lifelong dream of mine to write this book. No dream is ever actualized without the help of many people. Everyone should have an Aunt Mary Bee like I did. She believed in my notions to colorize digital media when the Macintosh computer was very young. My childhood friend, Marleane (Petesy) Owen, joined me at art museum adventures in our youth. This book is dedicated to my parents and I also had the good fortune to have a stepmother, Nancy Vosburgh Rhyne, who promoted my early concepts in K-12 computer graphics education. Judy Brown and Steve Cunningham oversaw my first K-12 computer graphics education grant through ACM SIGGAPH.

My 15 years in the Stanford University community, first as a student and later as a staff member in information technology, helped me to form the foundation of this book. I am indebted to the Palo Alto arts community for championing many of my early computer graphics art shows.

My 13 years as a government contractor with the U.S. Environmental Protection Agency (EPA) allowed me to gain fundamental visualization experiences. EPA Project Officer Walter Shackelford, championed our founding of the U.S. EPA Scientific Visualization Center. My 8 years at North Carolina State University were equally rewarding. Tom Miller and Mladen Vouk provided terrific opportunities in multimedia and visual analytics. Dan Reed and Alan Blatecky supported my setting up the Renaissance Computing Institute's Engagement Center at North Carolina State University. My collaborators at RENCI@NCSU—Jefferson Heard, Gary Lackmann, John Blondin, Melissa Pasquinelli, and Matt Evans— helped me to evolve colorization methods. I am specifically indebted to Steve Chall, Sidharth Thakur, and Chris Williams for our many RENCI@ NCSU visualization efforts.

Over the last 7 years, Chris Johnson at the Scientific Computing and Imaging Institute at the University of Utah, Kwan Liu Ma at the University of California at Davis, and Pat Hanrahan at Stanford University provided me with consulting opportunities to apply color theory to visualization. Sharon Lin allowed me to coach her on color theory during her PhD studies.

I very much appreciate Donna Anstey, who is at Yale University Press, for providing permission to use the various coloring examples that I created with the *Interaction of Color by Josef Albers* app in this book. Rick Adams, Jennifer Ahringer, Sherry Thomas, Iris Fahrer, as well as many others with the Taylor & Francis Group helped me to make publication of this book possible. Balasubramanian Shanmugam and his team at DiacriTech handled the manuscript editing and layout for the book. This book would not have evolved without the terrific online and mobile applications that I covered in this book. To all of the software development teams who built these color applications, thank you very much.

I am particularly indebted to my online friends who have shared with me their thoughts about our daily color studies.

In preparing this book, many people encouraged me. I especially thank Marta Fuchs and her brother, Henry Fuchs, who cheered me when I wrote the book proposal and completed each chapter. Mark Simpson-Voss coached me on publishing contracts and helped me understand fundamentals about book publishing. My cousin, Jane Ann Nelson, continues to champion me online with each color study. Judy Brown and Steve Chall read early versions of various chapters in this book and provided countless edits. Many *creatives* in the Apple Store at the Streets of Southpoint in Durham, North Carolina, taught me illustration techniques that appear in this book. Kim Biese of Papyrus at the Streets of Southpoint let me work for her and explore color schemes in greeting cards. Distant family members Carol Johnson, Billy Johnson, Sally B. Rich, "Aunt" Sarah Williams Britt, and Nanette Lewis Rhyne endured many conversations about this book. My neighbors, Elaine and Melvin Hinton, along with Reggie, Wendy, and Victoria Burnette checked in on me as I prepared content.

The majority of this book was written during my recovery from a set of serious medical conditions. I am indebted to many people at Duke Medical Center for a successful recovery. I specifically thank Michael A. Blazing, MD, Anuradha Sabapathi, MD, Daniel M. Kaplan, MD, Nick Kuntz, MD, Edward N. Rampersaud Jr., MD, Andrew D. Petterson, MD, John Eppensteiner, MD, Marc Samsky, MD, and Nilesh Patel, MD. My church family with the Triangle Presbyterian Church kept up their prayers and faith that I would recover. I also thank Donna Monzon, Beth Murphy,

Rev. Ray Cobb, Rev. Casey Clark, Colleen Loree, Missy Owen, Richard Valenti, Beverly Santos, Jeannie Phelps, Donna Myers, Judy Fleming, Sherene Min, MD, Roberta Vandalen, Nancy Holton, Helen Santos, Diane Albert, Andy Batton, Betsy Batton, Juliellen Simpson-Vos, Dawn Macelroy, and many others for being there when I genuinely needed it. Finally, I am most thankful for my relationship with God who shares His hope and love for me each day.

Theresa-Marie Rhyne
Durham, North Carolina

Author

Theresa-Marie Rhyne has over 25 years of experience in producing and colorizing digital media and visualization. She has consulted with the Stanford University Visualization Group on a color suggestion prototype system, the Center for Visualization at the University of California at Davis, and the Scientific Computing and Imaging Institute at the University of Utah on applying color theory to ensemble data visualization. Prior to her consulting work, she founded two visualization centers: (1) the United States Environmental Protection Agency's Scientific Visualization Center in the 1990s and (2) the Center for Visualization and Analytics at North Carolina State University in the 2000s. Theresa-Marie Rhyne earned a BS degree, two MS degrees, and the Degree of Engineer in Civil Engineering from Stanford University. She entered the computer graphics field as a result of her computational and geographic modeling research in geotechnical and earthquake engineering. She is also an internationally recognized digital media artist who began creating digital media with early Apple computers, including the colorization of early Macintosh educational software.

Her web site is www.theresamarierhyne.com and her blog is located at http://www.theresamarierhyne.com/Theresa-Marie_Rhynes_Viewpoint/Blog/Blog.html. Follow her on twitter at: @tmrhyne.

Introduction

COLOR RESULTS FROM OUR eyes' interaction with the light spectrum. For people with eyesight, color is a visual perceptual property of the environment and objects that surround us. Light, regardless of the complexity of its wavelengths, is reduced to three fundamental color components by the human eye. Our retinas contain three types of color receptor cells or cones. These components are long wavelength or red cones, medium wavelength or green cones, and short wavelength or blue cones. Our eyes are wired to understand color in terms of Red, Green, and Blue. However, our brain also gets involved with color perception to make human color vision more intriguing. As a result, when color captured from our eyes travels via the optic nerve to our brain, Red and Green lights can combine to produce a Yellow color. This seems unbelievable to us because when we mix Red and Green paints, as we did in kindergarten, we obtain a Gray paint. If we use a color printer, Yellow is a one of the inks and no mixing is required to obtain the color. This is because the color models are different in all three cases. The color model for lights or displays is Red, Green, and Blue, while the color model for paint pigments is Red, Yellow, and Blue. The color model for printing with inks is Cyan, Magenta, Yellow, and Key (Black). Additionally, the appearance of a color changes according to its context and is influenced by the other hues and lighting surrounding it. Working with color is complicated and not always intuitive.

A body of knowledge, called color theory, has evolved over the centuries to provide guidance in visual effects and mixing of color combinations. These color management challenges are just some of the many components presented in this book, *Applying Color Theory to Digital Media and Visualization*. We demonstrate how the interrelationships of color principles influence the process of creating color schemes and imagery. We discuss visual simulation tools that indicate how individuals with color deficiencies might view specific color images. Working with online and mobile color evaluation tools, we show how to analyze a color scheme from an existing digital image and save it for future application. Using the color wheel representation, we define the fundamentals of color harmony and highlight how to use these concepts in visual content creation. We provide practical approaches that you can use in your own efforts to create digital media and visualizations. Figure I.1 shows a visual overview of the concepts covered in our discussions.

In this book, we have capitalized colors. As an example, rather than writing "yellow," we write "Yellow" to note the importance of colors in our discussions. We also provide many references for further reading on topics. We note URLs to access an online color tool or find information about acquiring a particular mobile app. In Chapter 7, we provide both a text summary and visual collage of selected illustrations for each prior chapter in this book.

We use the color tools and techniques presented in these chapters on a daily basis. Every day, I enjoy exploring a new aspect of color theory and actively belong to social media sites for sharing color work. Relationships with colleagues at Adobe Color's social media site and the COLOURlovers

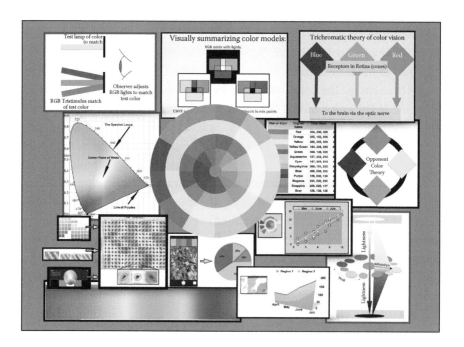

FIGURE I.1   Visual summary of highlights from *Applying Color Theory to Digital Media and Visualization*. Illustration by Theresa-Marie Rhyne, 2016.

online creative community, in particular, as well as comments from Twitter and Facebook postings, were very helpful in developing a number of the concepts presented here. So, let us get started on our journey of color exploration.

CHAPTER 1

Introduction to Color Models

A COLOR MODEL IS A structured system for creating a full range of colors from a small set of defined primary colors. There are three fundamental models of color theory. As shown in Figure 1.1, these models are as follows: (1) the Red, Green, and Blue (RGB) color model of lights and display originally explored by Isaac Newton in 1666; (2) the Cyan, Magenta, Yellow, and Key Black (CMYK) model for printing in color originally patented by Jacob Christoph Le Blon in 1719; and (3) the Red, Yellow, Blue painters model fully summarized by Johann Wolfgang von Goethe in 1810 [1]. Figure 1.1 shows a visual summary of these three fundamental models of color theory.

1.1 THE RGB COLOR MODEL

As shown in Figure 1.2, the RGB color model assembles the primary lights of Red, Green, and Blue together in various combinations to produce a broad range of colors. Red and Green lights are combined together to produce Yellow light. The RGB color model is termed as an additive color model in which the combination of the Red, Green, and Blue primary lights produces White light. The RGB color model is used in various technologies producing color images, such as conventional photography and the display of images in electronic systems. Examples of the RGB input devices include image scanners, video games, and digital cameras as well

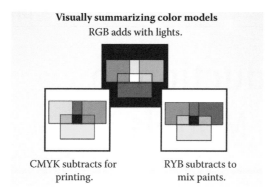

FIGURE 1.1   Visual summary of color models. The Red, Green, and Blue (RGB) color model is an additive color model for displays. The Cyan, Magenta, Yellow, and Key Black (CMYK) color model is a subtractive color model for printing. The Red, Yellow, and Blue (RYB) color model is designed for mixing colors with paints. (Images created by Theresa-Marie Rhyne, 2016.)

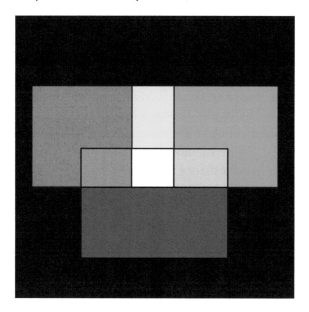

FIGURE 1.2   Illustration of the RGB color model. (Image created by Theresa-Marie Rhyne, 2016.)

as television and video cameras. RGB output devices encompass the broad range of television-set technologies and video projector systems, along with computer and mobile phone displays. The RGB color model has a solid logic in terms of physics and the human perception of colors. Next, we provide a historical overview of this logic.

In 1666, Isaac Newton explored the dispersion of White sunlight into a rainbow of colors. His experiments involved holding a glass prism in the path of sunlight coming through a hole in a dark room. The White light split into Red, Orange, Yellow, Green, Blue (actually Cyan), Indigo (frequently referred to as Dark Blue), and Violet. Newton asserted that different colors combined to produce the White light. Newton published his findings in a book entitled *Opticks*, in English, in 1704 [2]. Newton's rainbow color map for light has become the fundamental approach in the design of today's visualization and digital media presentations. Newton also developed the initial concept of the color wheel that we will highlight in Section 1.4 of this chapter on color models. Although Newton did not define Red, Green, and Blue as the primary colors, his research was the first step in showing that color lights combine together to produce a broad array of additional colors. In Figure 1.3a, we diagram the conventional arrangement of what Newton defined as the dispersion of the

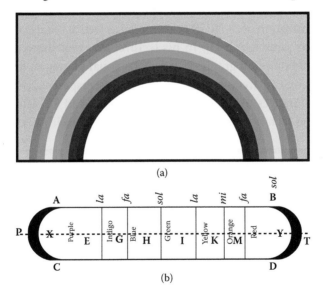

FIGURE 1.3 (a) Rainbow diagram showing the conventional arrangement of colors (Red, Orange, Yellow, Green, Blue [actually Cyan], Indigo [Dark Blue], and Violet). (Based on Newton, I., *Opticks: or a Treatise of the Reflexions, Refractions, Inflexions and Colours of Light*, Samuel Smith and Benjamin Walford, London, United Kingdom, 1704. Image created by Theresa-Marie Rhyne, 2016.) (b) Redrawing of Isaac Newton's diagram of the spectrum of light. (Adapted from Newton, I., *Opticks: or a Treatise of the Reflexions, Refractions, Inflexions and Colours of Light*, Samuel Smith and Benjamin Walford, London, United Kingdom, 1704. Image created by Theresa-Marie Rhyne, 2016.)

White light into a rainbow of colors. In Figure 1.3b, we show an adapted version of Newton's original drawing of the spectrum of colors from his book *Opticks* in 1704. Newton's notations in the diagram refer to an analogy he developed where the seven colors of the rainbow correspond to the musical concept of seven sound intervals displayed by an octave.

The RGB color model was actually defined in regard to the theory of trichromatic color vision. In 1802, Thomas Young, in a lecture entitled *On the Theory of Light and Colours*, postulated that each human eye had three types of photoreceptors (today referred to as cone cells). Young further proposed that each photoreceptor is sensitive to specific ranges of the visible light. In 1851, Hermann von Helmholtz, in his book *Treatise on Physiological Optics*, added to the theory further by noting that the three types of cone photoreceptors are long preferring (Red), medium preferring (Green), and short preferring (Blue). We will highlight these color vision concepts further in Chapter 2.

In 1861, during a lecture on his color studies at the Royal Institute in the United Kingdom, James Clerk Maxwell provided the first widely recognized demonstration of the RGB color model as well as what is often called the first color photograph [3]. In his lecture, Maxwell showed an image of a tartan ribbon photographed by a professional photographer on three plates through Red, Green, and Blue-Violet filters, respectively. Combining these filtered images together onto a screen produced a reasonable color display of the tartan ribbon. Figure 1.4 shows Maxwell's demonstration

FIGURE 1.4   Image of a tartan ribbon that James Clerk Maxwell demonstrated in his 1861 lecture on the RGB color model. This image is also considered the *first color photograph*. (From Maxwell, J.C., *Br. J. Photogr.*, August 9, 1861, public domain.)

that was revolutionary in 1861. This concept is now used in present-day video projection systems and is fundamental in regard to television, video, computer, and mobile phone displays.

1.2 THE CMYK COLOR MODEL

The CMYK color model is designed to support color printing on White paper. The CMYK color model is termed as a subtractive color model in which the starting point begins with a White or light surface. Color pigments reduce the reflection of the original White light. The color inks thus *subtract* from the original White surface. Typical output devices for the CMYK color model include color inkjet, laser, and dye-sublimation printers. Each device has its own particular technology for color image reproduction. Figure 1.5 shows the CMYK color model.

Historically, for color printing processes to work, individual plates were created for the Cyan, Magenta, and Yellow (CMY) color pigments. The plates were registered over top of each other to produce full color images and the process was called a three-color printing process. When the primary pigments of CMY were combined together as inks, in equally large

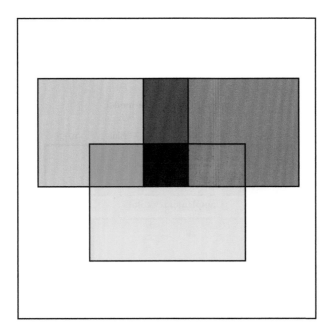

FIGURE 1.5   Illustration of the CMYK color model. (Image created by Theresa-Marie Rhyne, 2016.)

amounts, the result was a Black color. When color printing was put into practice, combining the CMY inks together became an expensive process and, in some situations, certain papers were unable to absorb all of the ink required. As a result, the color printing process was modified to allow for a Black plate to support the printing of Black text and other Black elements with the CMY printing plates being registered or "keyed" against the Black plate. This color printing process and its associated model was thus termed the CMYK color model. CMYK is thus a four-color printing process.

Today, when a digital image is printed, the RGB numeric values of the image are converted to the CMYK numeric values of a printer. In theory, the RGB and CMYK color models are complementary to each other. Various combinations of the Red, Green, and Blue primaries of the RGB color model produce CMY. The reverse is true for the CMY primaries where combinations of the CMYK color model produce Red, Green, and Blue. In practice, these combinations are not purely complementary since the RGB color model involves lights and the CMYK color model involves pigments. Colors selected and matched on an RGB mobile phone can appear with different intensity, perhaps even more subdued, when reproduced on White paper via a CMYK ink jet printer. Figure 1.6 shows the complementary relationship between the RGB and CMYK color models.

Three- and four-color reproduction processes were first patented in 1719 by Jacob Christoph Le Blon. Le Blon actually used Red, Yellow, and Blue (RYB) inks on individual metal plates with a Key Black registration plate as

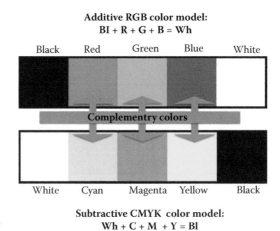

FIGURE 1.6   Diagram of the complementary relationship between the RGB color model and CMYK model. (Image created by Theresa-Marie Rhyne, 2016.)

the foundation for his color reproduction methods. Like the CMYK color model, the RYB color model is also a subtractive model. We will highlight the RYB painters color model in the following section.

1.3 THE RYB COLOR MODEL

The RYB color model is a subtractive color model for mixing painting pigments. It is usually the first color model that we learn at an early age, perhaps in kindergarten. Starting with White paper, RYB color pigments when combined together yield Black, similar to the CMYK color model. Secondary colors that result from mixing primary pigments include the following: (1) the combination of Red and Yellow to yield Orange, (2) the combination of Yellow and Blue to yield Green, and (3) the combination of Blue and Red to yield Purple. The RYB color model is used in the arts and arts education. Figure 1.7 shows the RYB color model.

As discussed previously, Newton published his rainbow color map findings in 1704. During that period, production and reproduction of color images was performed with paint pigments on a White or cream canvas. Painters relied on the RYB color model for mixing and understanding colors. The theory of trichromatic (RGB) color vision had not been postulated. Although mirror displays existed, photographic, television, video, computer, and mobile display technologies with Red, Green, and Blue lights had not been developed. The RYB color model of the eighteenth century was the foundation of theories of color vision.

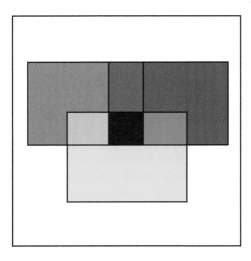

FIGURE 1.7 Illustration of the RYB color model. (Image created by Theresa-Marie Rhyne, 2016.)

As a result, it was difficult for painters to understand how to incorporate Newton's observation (dispersion of White sunlight into a rainbow of colors) into their working knowledge of the RYB color theory. Therefore, Newton's observations were very misunderstood and frequently challenged by painters and other visual artists in the eighteenth century. It was not until the nineteenth-century developments of RGB color vision principles that the relationship between additive and subtractive color models, as shown in Figure 1.6, was understood. In the following section, we will highlight the evolution of color theory based on the color wheel concepts introduced by Newton and later modified by eighteenth-century artists and scientists.

1.4 OVERVIEW OF THE HISTORICAL PROGRESSION OF COLOR THEORY

As noted in Section 1.1, Isaac Newton developed the initial concept of the color circle or the color wheel. His diagram, shown in Figure 1.8, was published in his 1704 book, entitled *Opticks*. Newton transitioned individual spectral colors, observed in his prism experiments, into a closed color circle. He selected seven colors to correspond to the musical concept of seven sound intervals displayed by an octave. Newton decisions on specific colors were based on aesthetic preferences rather than on scientific principles. He chose Red, Orange, Yellow, Green, Blue (actually Cyan), Indigo (frequently referred to as dark Blue), and Violet. Newton's *Opticks* book went on to become one of the most widely read scientific books of the eighteenth century. His rainbow color map concepts and establishment of the color circle or color wheel continue to influence us even today. In Section 2.11 of Chapter 2, we will highlight some of the difficulties in using the rainbow or Newtonian color map as a default color scheme for current visualization and visual analytics efforts.

In 1766, over 60 years after Isaac Newton's writings on the color circle, Moses Harris published his *Natural System of Colours* book. Moses Harris was an entomologist and engraver in England [4]. In his book, Harris described the RYB color model and demonstrated the wide variety of colors that resulted from combinations of the three primary colors. His observations built upon the writings of Newton as well as Jacob Christoph Le Blon's patented three-color separation printing process of 1719. Harris was particularly focused on the classification of colors and the relationships between specific colors. As a result, he made the first known published attempt to diagram the RYB color wheel. He defined

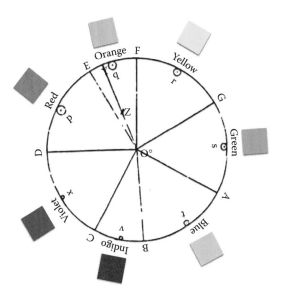

FIGURE 1.8 Adapted from Isaac Newton's Color Circle diagram that appeared in his 1704 *Opticks* book. We have added color squares to highlight Newton's text descriptions of colors noted in the circle diagram. (Adapted from Newton, I., *Opticks: or, a Treatise of the Reflexions, Refractions, Inflexions and Colours of Light*, Samuel Smith and Benjamin Walford, London, United Kingdom, 1704. Image adapted by Theresa-Marie Rhyne, 2016.)

a *prismatic* or primary color wheel for Red, Yellow, and Blue as well as a *compound* color wheel for the secondary colors of Orange, Green, and Purple. Harris' color wheels were divided into arc segments to diagram pure colors as well as shades and tones. At the center of the wheel, the three primaries mix together to form Black. This would later be defined as a subtractive color model. Scientists, artists, and engravers valued Harris' color wheel since it served as a simplified and practical way to quickly visualize the relationships among colors and allowed for matching colors to existing samples. Figure 1.9 shows Moses Harris' prismatic and compound color wheels.

In 1810, Johann Wolfgang von Goethe published *Zur Farbenlehre* (translated into English as *Theory of Colours*) that became the foundation for color theory in regard to the RYB color model. In his book, Goethe challenged many of Newton's writings on the physics of color and introduced a systematic exploration of the physiological and psychological effects of color. Goethe proposed a symmetric color wheel composed of colors that oppose or complement each other. His writings discussed how

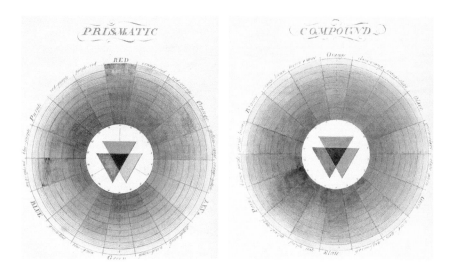

FIGURE 1.9 The prismatic and compound color wheels published by Moses Harris. The natural system of colors. Leicester–Fields: Laidler; 1766. (From Harris, M., *The Natural System of Colours*, Laidler, Leicester Fields, London, 1766, public domain.)

complementary colors cancel each other out to produce Gray or Black when mixed as pigments. He also noted that when two opposing colors are placed next to each other, humans perceive the highest or strongest contrast for these two particular colors. His diagram, shown in Figure 1.10, included Yellow opposing Violet, Orange opposing Blue, and Green opposing Magenta. The inclusion of Magenta by Goethe was a departure from the Newtonian views of color. Magenta is a nonspectral color and thus was not included in Newton's definition of fundamental colors. Goethe viewed Magenta as the mixture of Violet and Red that completed the color circle or the color wheel. The role that Goethe defined for Magenta is still applied today in modern color systems. He also intentionally recognized the psychological effect of Magenta appearing as an afterimage resulting from intensely viewing Green. Figure 1.10 shows Johann Wolfgang von Goethe's color wheel of complementary or opposing colors.

Goethe's book was a catalog of his color studies and observations. He also noted Red and Green as complementary pigments in regard to the RYB color model. It appears Goethe slightly merged additive color concepts of what later became the RGB color model of lights with subtractive concepts of the RYB color model of pigments in his many observations. These kinds of inconsistencies and Goethe's direct attack on Newton's

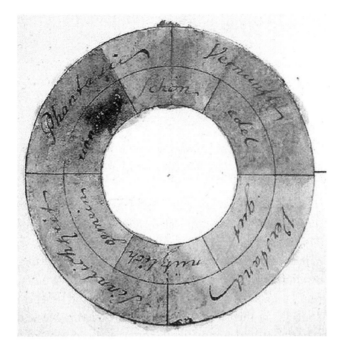

FIGURE 1.10   Johann Wolfgang von Goethe's color wheel. (From Wolfgang von Goethe, J., *Goethe's Theory of Colours*, Translated with notes by C. L. Eastlake, R.A. F.R.S., John Murray, London, United Kingdom, 1840, public domain.)

color observations resulted in scientists dismissing many aspects of Goethe's book. In 1840, Charles Eastlake published an English translation of Goethe's *Zur Farbenlehre* book and entitled it *Theory of Colours*. Eastlake, in his English version, omitted many of Goethe's statements that challenged Newton's color observations. This allowed the reader to focus more directly on the physiological and psychological color studies noted by Goethe. Painters embraced Eastlake's translation of *Goethe's Theory of Colours*. Goethe's writings went on to become widely adopted as one of the foundations of color theory by the visual arts community.

In 1824, Michel Chevreul, a highly regarded French chemist, was appointed as the director of the dyeing department at the Gobelin Tapestry factory. His chief task was to investigate the causes of fading in tapestry threads. Chevreul realized that the difficulties were not with the dyes, but rather with simultaneous color contrast between adjacent threads. After 4 years of study, in 1828, Chevreul published his first paper on his observations, entitled *Memoir on the influence that two colours can have on each other when seen simultaneously*. In 1839, after much effort to achieve effective color reproduction of his

FIGURE 1.11 Example of simultaneous contrast between Orange and Cyan (Light Blue) squares. (Image created by Theresa-Marie Rhyne, 2016.)

diagrams, Chevreul published his book *De la Loi du Contraste Simultané des Couleurs*. The French book was translated into German, English, and other languages [5]. In 1854, Charles Martel published an English translation entitled *The Principles of Harmony and Contrast of Colours, and their Application to the Arts*. Additionally, Chevreul went on to publish three other books on color. Chevreul's books were widely read by painters and others artists who applied his concepts in their image creation and design processes. His writings on color harmony and simultaneous contrast are considered part of the foundations of color theory that are still applied today. Figure 1.11 provides an example of Chevreul's principle of simultaneous contrast.

For this example, I consider Orange and Cyan squares placed next to each other and inside each other. These hues have high contrast according to the RYB color model. Notice that the Cyan (light Blue) square on the Orange background appears larger than the Orange square on the Cyan background. These two colors also appear to amplify or intensify each other when the colors are viewed together. The viewer perceives these colors as altered; however, the hues have not actually changed. These are some of the simultaneous contrast principles that Chevreul presented in his books.

In his writings on color, Chevreul diagramed a color wheel with 12 main color units of Red, Reddish Orange, Orange, Orange Yellow, Yellow, Yellowish Green, Green, Greenish Blue, Blue, Violet Blue, Violet, and Violet Red, with six zones in each color unit. This resulted in a total of 72 segments for his color wheel based on the RYB color model. Complementary (e.g., intensely contrasting) colors were placed directly opposite to each other on the color wheel. Chevreul called this color wheel a *chromatic diagram*. I show an example from his first book on *The Principles of Harmony and Contrast of Colours, and their Application to the Arts* in Figure 1.12.

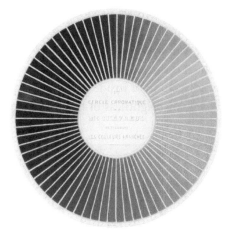

FIGURE 1.12 Michel Eugène Chevreul's color wheel or chromatic diagram that emphasizes complementary (opposing) colors. (From Chevreul, M.E., *De la loi du contraste simultané des couleurs et de l'assortiment des objets colorés*, Translated by C. Martel as *The Principles of Harmony and Contrast of Colours*, Longman, Brown, Green and Longmans, London, 1839, public domain.)

1.5 AN EXAMPLE OF COLOR THEORY APPLICATION

Here, we highlight an example of the application of our simultaneous contrast knowledge to a visualization problem. Our task is to develop a color scheme for a *treemap* visualization. In the field of Information Visualization, a treemap permits the display of hierarchical data by creating a set of nested squares. Each branch of the tree is defined with a rectangle and tiled with smaller rectangles that represent sub branches. Color and size dimensions of rectangles are correlated with the tree structure. This allows seeing patterns in the data that would be challenging to detect in other ways. Treemaps can effectively display thousands of items simultaneously. Ben Shneiderman at the University of Maryland's Human–Computer Interaction Lab invented the treemap visualization method in the 1990s [6]. Returning to our task of building a color scheme for a treemap visualization, I recall that the artist Petit Mondrian also worked in squares and rectangles. In his paintings, Mondrian preferred to use the primary colors of the RYB color model [7]. Figure 1.13 shows a color display structure similar to the paintings of Mondrian that I created with Paletton's Color Scheme Designer [8]. Color Scheme Designer is an online tool for creating color schemes that I will discuss further in Chapter 5.

For our treemap visualization, we need two colors and decide to apply an Orange and Cyan (light Blue) complementary color structure noted in Goethe's writings. However, I recall the concepts of simultaneous contrast noted by Chevreul, which is shown in Figure 1.11. As a result, I do not place these colors precisely adjacent to or inside each other, vary sizes of the rectangles, and reduce the color brightness of the color selections. Figure 1.14

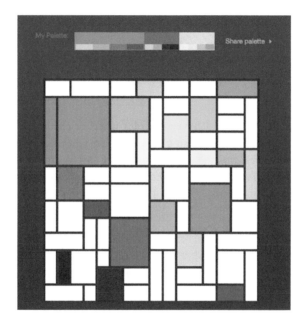

FIGURE 1.13   An RYB color scheme design using a display structure similar to the paintings of Petit Mondrian. I used Paletton's Color Scheme Designer to create this image. (Based on Paletton, Color Scheme Designer, Available at http://www.paletton.com, 2016. Image created by Theresa-Marie Rhyne, 2016.)

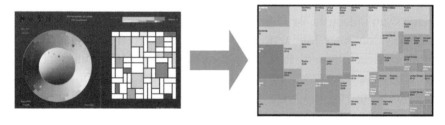

FIGURE 1.14   An example of color theory application using an Orange and Cyan complementary color scheme. (Based on Paletton Color Scheme Designer, available at http://www.paletton.com, 2016; and Tableu Public Software, available at https://public.tableau.com/s/, 2016. Image created by Theresa-Marie Rhyne, 2015.)

shows the Mondrain-like Orange and Cyan color map created with Color Scheme Designer on the left. On the right, in Figure 1.14, I show the application of the Orange and Cyan color scheme to a treemap visualization created with Tableau Public Software (https://public.tableau.com/s/). Tableau Public Software is a freely available tool for building visualizations, especially from tabular data. Tableau Software Inc. provides this free version, with limited functionality, in addition to their commercially available products [9].

1.6 CONCLUDING REMARKS

In this chapter, I reviewed the following three key color models: (1) the RGB color model for displays, (2) the CMYK color model for printing, and (3) the RYB color model for paints. Next, I provided a brief overview of the historical progression of color theory. I will revisit the historical evolution of the color wheel and color harmony in Chapter 4. In Chapter 2, I will focus on color vision concepts that are key to furthering our understanding of the RGB color model for displays.

REFERENCES

1. Wolfgang von Goethe, J. (1840), *Goethe's Theory of Colours.* Translated with notes by C. L. Eastlake, R.A. F.R.S. London, United Kingdom: John Murray. Available at https://archive.org/details/goethestheoryco01goetgoog, accessed June 4, 2016.
2. Newton, I. (1704). *Opticks: or a Treatise of the Reflexions, Refractions, Inflexions, and Colours of Light.* Also *Two Treatises of the Species and Magnituder of Curvilinear Figures* and *The Project Gutenberg EBook of Opticks.* London, United Kingdom: Samuel Smith and Benjamin Walford. Available at http://www.gutenberg.org/files/33504/33504-h/33504-h.htm, accessed June 4, 2016.
3. Maxwell, J. C. (1861). The theory of the Primary Colors. *The British Journal of Photography,* August 9, 1861. Available at http://notesonphotographs .org/index.php?title=%22The_Theory_of_the_Primary_Colours.%22_The _British_Journal_of_Photography,_August_9,_1861, accessed June 4, 2016.
4. Harris, M. (1766). *The Natural System of Colours.* Leicester Fields, London: Laidler.
5. Eugène Chevreul, M. (1839). *De la loi du contraste simultané des couleurs et de l'assortiment des objets colorés.* Translated by C. Martel as *The Principles of Harmony and Contrast of Colours.* London, United Kingdom: Longman, Brown, Green and Longmans.
6. Johnson, B. and Shneiderman, B. (1991). Tree-maps: A Space-Filling Approach to the Visualization of Hierarchical Information Structures.

Proceedings of the IEEE Conference on Visualization, 1991. San Diego, CA, IEEE, pp. 284–291.

7. Mondrian, P. (1986). The new art—The new life: The collected writings of Piet Mondrian. In H. Holtzman and M. S. James (eds.), *Documents of 20th-Century Art*, Boston, MA: G. K. Hall. Reprinted 1987, London: Thames and Hudson. Reprinted 1993, New York, NY: Da Capo Press, pp. 224–230.

8. Paletton. 2016. Color Scheme Designer. Available at http://www.paletton .com; accessed on March 8, 2016.

9. Tableau Software. 2016. Tableau Public Software. Available at https://public .tableau.com/s/; accessed on March 8, 2016.

CHAPTER 2

Review of Color Vision Principles

2.1 VISIBLE LIGHT SPECTRUM

In the scientific terms, color is both a psychological and physiological response to light waves of specific frequencies that strike our eyes. Human eyes are sensitive to a narrow subset of the broad range of frequencies in the electromagnetic spectrum. This is called the *visible light* spectrum. Visible light, detectable by humans, ranges from wavelengths of approximately 390–780 nm [1]. Specific wavelengths within the visible light spectrum correspond to the specific colors. As discussed in Chapter 1, Isaac Newton defined the visible spectrum as ranging from short wavelengths of Violet to long wavelengths of Red with Indigo (Dark Blue), Blue (actually Cyan), and Green, Yellow, and Orange being the colors in between. Figure 2.1 shows the approximate range of wavelengths that correspond to perceived colors in the visible light spectrum. Figure 2.1 begins with the short waves of Violet and ends with the long waves of Red. This representation does not specify the Indigo color, between Violet and Blue, that Newton noted in his original writings.

2.2 HUMAN VISION FUNDAMENTALS

The key biological components of vision are the eye, the visual center in the brain, and the optic nerve that connects the two. Light enters the eye through the pupil. Behind the pupil of the eye is the lens. The lens behaves similar to a camera lens. In conjunction with the eye's cornea, the lens

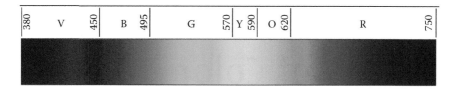

FIGURE 2.1 Representation of the visible light spectrum. This diagram moves from short waves of 380 nm in the Violet range to 750 nm in the Red range. The colors span from Violet, Blue, Green, Yellow, Orange, and Red. Color ranges were specified according to the *CRC Handbook of Fundamental Spectroscopic Correlation Charts*. (From Gringer, 2008, https://commons.wikimedia.org/wiki/File:Linear_visible_spectrum.svg, in the public domain by request of the creator.)

adjusts the focal length of the image that strikes the inside surface of the eye called the retina. The lens of the eye reverses images as it focuses on them. The direct images on the retina are upside down and the visual center of the brain flips the images back over to interpret what we see. Figure 2.2 shows the anatomy of the eye. In addition to the key components for vision, Figure 2.2 also notes the conjunctiva that lines the inside of the eyelid and covers the sclera (the White part) of the eye as well as the iris that controls the diameter and size of the pupil. The iris controls the amount of light reaching the retina and the color of the iris gives the eye its color.

The retina is lined with rods and cones that serve as light sensors and are called photoreceptor cells. Combined, the rods and cones cover the complete range of the eye's adaption to light. Together, they gather the information that our brain interprets into one combined image. The rods are sensitive to the intensity of light, but do not distinguish between lights of varying wavelengths. The rods are located at the edge of the retina and work in dim light to provide a coarse sketch of the world around us. The rods are far more numerous than cones, but are out of commission in bright light. The cones are clustered at the center of the retina, called the fovea, and work in bright light. The cones are the color-sensing cells of the retina and are responsible for our ability to see fine detail. When light of a specific wavelength enters the pupil and strikes the cones of the retina, a chemical reaction results with the optic nerve sending electrical impulses to the brain. The brain interprets these electrical impulses of the cones as various colors [2].

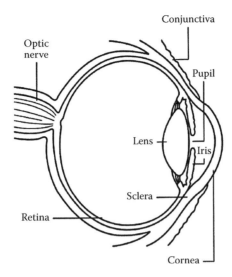

FIGURE 2.2   Anatomy of the eye. The vision process in humans involves light entering the eye through the pupil and then striking the inside surface of the eye called the retina. (From The National Eye Institute, National Institutes of Health, United States of America, July 10, 2012, https://www.flickr.com/photos/nationaleyeinstitute/7544655864, public domain.)

2.3 TRICHROMATIC COLOR VISION

Color vision is thus a function of the cones. The theory of *trichromatic* color vision asserts that there are three types of cones and each is optimized to absorb a different spectrum range of the visible light [3]. The first set of cones absorbs long waves of light in the Red range. The second set of cones absorbs middle waves of light in the Green range. The third set of cones absorbs short waves of light in the Blue range. We covered the contributions of Thomas Young and Hermann von Helmholtz to the theory of trichromatic color vision in the discussion of the Red, Green, and Blue (RGB) color model in Chapter 1. As noted, James Clerk Maxwell's demonstration of the RGB color model during his 1861 lecture at the Royal Institute in the United Kingdom was considered the "proof" of Young's and Helmholtz's assertions. Figure 2.3 shows a diagram of the theory of trichromatic color vision. In Figure 2.3, the Blue cones with short wavelengths are shown on the left, the Green cones with medium wavelengths are shown in the middle, and the Red cones with longer wavelengths are shown on the right. This corresponds to the left to right progression of the visible light spectrum shown in Figure 2.1.

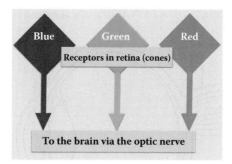

FIGURE 2.3   Diagram of the *trichromatic* theory of color vision. The Blue cones that handle short wavelengths are shown on the left, the Green cones that handle medium wavelengths are shown in the middle, and the Red cones that handle long wavelengths are shown on the right. This corresponds to the left to right progression of the visible light spectrum shown previously in Figure 2.1. (Illustration by Theresa-Marie Rhyne, 2015.)

2.4 OPPONENT COLOR THEORY

In 1878, Ewald Hering, a German physiologist, published *Outlines of a Theory of the Light Sense* in which he challenged the Young and Helmholtz theory of the trichromatic color vision [4]. Hering opposed the purely physiological understanding of the RGB color model. Hering proposed that color vision occurred in three channels where opposite colors are in competition. The channels are as follows: (1) a Red Green channel, (2) a Yellow Blue channel, and (3) a Black White channel. The Black White channel, or achromatic system, addresses brightness contrast. Together, the Red Green channel and Yellow Blue channel create a chromatic system for color contrast. Hering postulated that there were four primary colors with Red and Green opposing each other and Yellow and Blue opposing each other. In his writings, Hering noted that we do not see Reddish Green combinations of color. The same is true for Yellow and Blue and we do not see Yellowish Blue combinations of color. Figure 2.4 shows Hering's *opponent color theory*.

The assertion that Yellow was a primary color was controversial given the wide acceptance of the trichromatic color vision in the late 1800s scientific community. Hering's premise was that our psychological experience produces four distinct color hues from which all other colors are mixed. Hering based some of his opponent processing theory on color afterimages. For example, Red and Green are opposite colors. If we focus our vision on a Red dot and then gaze at a White wall, we will see a Green dot as an afterimage. Reversely, if we focus on a Green dot and gaze at a

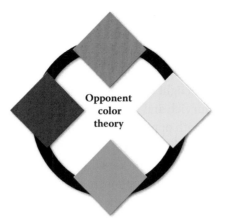

FIGURE 2.4 *Opponent* color theory concept. (Illustration by Theresa-Marie Rhyne, 2015.)

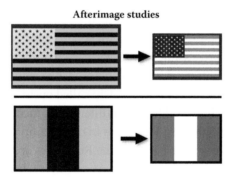

FIGURE 2.5 Examples of afterimage studies. Stare at each individual image on the left for 60 seconds and look away to a blank wall. The results should be the images on the right. (Public Domain images and examples, redrawn by Theresa-Marie Rhyne, 2016.)

White wall, we will see a Red dot afterimage. The same results occur for Blue and Yellow. Figure 2.5 shows two examples of afterimage studies.

Ewald Hering and Hermann von Helmholtz were contemporaries who argued intensely regarding the differences between the trichromatic color vision and opponent processing color theory. Each viewpoint appeared to have credibility in explaining some aspects of color vision. In 1957, while doing work for Eastman Kodak, Leo Hurvich and Dorothea Jameson provided quantitative data to support Hering's opponent processing color theory. Hurvich and Jameson defined the concept of *hue cancellation methods* [5]. Their research showed the following findings: (1) Red and Green lights mixed together produce Yellow light, not Reddish Green; (2) Blue and Yellow lights mixed together produce White light, not Yellowish Blue; and (3) Red and Green cancel each other, as do Yellow and Blue. Their findings also noted that starting with Blueish Green, it is possible to mix Yellow light with Blueish Green light to cancel out Blue. This results in the production of Green light. Hurvich and Jameson also showed that the trichromatic color vision coexisted with opponent processing color theory [5]. Helmholtz and Hering both had valid theories of color vision. Young and Helmholtz's theory of trichromatic color vision explains what happens with our eyes at the photoreceptor level. Hering's opponent processing color theory explains aspects of color vision processing at the neural level when images are transferred from the eye to the brain via the optic nerve.

2.5 TRICHROMACY, METAMERISM, AND COLOR CONSTANCY

As we have shown, the operation of our three cones is more complex than the RGB color model might indicate with trichromatic color vision coexisting with opponent processing color theory. Each of the retina's three types of cones contains a different kind of a photosensitive pigment. The pigments are composed of a transmembrane protein called opsin and a light-sensitive molecule called 11-*cis* retinal [6]. Each different pigment is sensitive to certain wavelengths of light. The Red cones in our eyes are sensitive to a range of long wavelengths. This means that the Red cones are not only activated by wavelengths of Red light, but, to a lesser extent, can be activated by wavelengths of Orange, Yellow, and even Green lights. Interestingly, the Red cones have their peak sensitivity in the Green to Yellow range of the visible spectrum. The Green cones, while being most sensitive to medium wavelengths of Green light, can also be activated by Yellow and Blue lights. The Green cones have their peak sensitivity in the Green wavelength range. The Blue cones are sensitive to short wavelengths of Violet and Blue lights and have their peak sensitivity in Violet to Blue wavelength zone. The responses of the three types of cones to light are called physiological responses. *Trichromacy* is the technical term for the condition of having three independent channels for conveying color information to our brain. Figure 2.6 shows the spectral sensitivity curves of our three types of cones to help depict the response to light as it strikes the retina [7].

The response of a specific type of cone varies by wavelength and intensity of the light. This information is transferred by the optic nerve to the brain. The brain is unable to discriminate different colors with input from

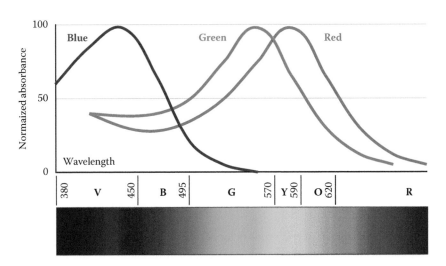

FIGURE 2.6 Spectral sensitivity curve diagrams for long-wave cone (Red), medium-wave cone (Green), and short-wave cone (Blue) responses. (Color spectrum image from Gringer, 2008, https://commons.wikimedia.org/wiki /File:Linear_visible_spectrum.svg, in the public domain by request of the creator.) (Spectral sensitivity curves adapted from Bowmaker, J.K. and Dartnall, H.J.A., *J. Physiol.*, 298, 1980, and drawn by Theresa-Marie Rhyne, 2015.)

only one type of cone. The interaction between at least two types of cones is needed for the brain to have the capability to perceive color. With information from at least two types of cones, the brain compares the signals from each type of cone and assesses the intensity and color of the light. Humans have three types of cones to support this activity. The brain's processing of the electrical messages sent by all three types of cones is called the psychological response to light. The sensitivity of our cones to long, medium, and short wavelengths is used to define the concept of long, medium, and short (LMS) color space. LMS color space is useful in the study of color deficiencies where one or more cone types are defective. We will cover color deficiencies in Section 2.8.

We work through an example of Yellow light to help clarify the concepts associated with trichromacy. Let us assume that a set of Yellow wavelengths (in the range of 577–597 nm) enters the eye and strikes the retina. Light with these wavelengths then activates the Red and Green sets of cones to produce the physiological response of electrical messages. The optical nerve sends the electrical messages to the brain. The brain then recognizes that Red and Green cones were simultaneously activated and interprets this to mean that the color Yellow was observed. The lack of

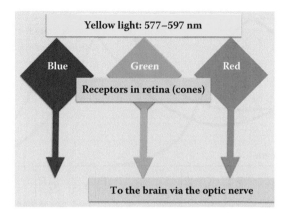

FIGURE 2.7 Diagram of *trichromacy* for a Yellow light example. Humans have three independent channels for conveying color information to the brain and this is called *trichromacy*. For a Yellow light, only the Green and Red channels operate. (Illustration by Theresa-Marie Rhyne, 2015.)

response from the Blue cones confirms this interpretation even further. Figure 2.7 diagrams these trichromacy concepts for a Yellow light example. As we noted in Section 2.4 when describing opponent processing color theory, we do not see Yellow and Blue together. This is the psychological response to the Yellow light [6].

We can also add complexity to this example by addressing the mixing of two different visible light wavelengths. If we send lights of Red and Green wavelengths to the eye simultaneously, the Red light would primarily activate the Red cones and the Green light would primarily activate the Green cones. Each set of cones would send their physiological messages to the brain via the optical nerve. The brain, trained to perceive the two simultaneous Red and Green signals to mean Yellow, would send a psychological response indicating that Yellow light has been received. The brain has no means of distinguishing between a set of single Yellow wavelengths and a set of Red and Green wavelengths combined. The combination of Red and Green lights to produce the equivalent of Yellow light is an example of the principle of *metamerism* [8]. Metamerism for color is generally defined as the matching of the apparent color of an object (for our case, Yellow) with spectral power distributions that are different from one another (for our case, Red and Green). Figure 2.8 diagrams the concept of metamerism for a Yellow light.

Metamerism is a key concept in working with the RGB color model that is discussed in Chapter 1. The combination of RGB lights to create

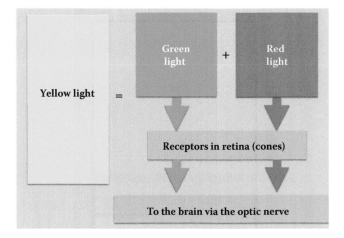

FIGURE 2.8   Diagram of *metamerism* for a Yellow light example. (Illustration by Theresa-Marie Rhyne, 2015.)

a combined color value is used in displays for electronic systems, such as digital cameras, televisions, computer and mobile phone displays, and video projectors [8]. For these displays, each pixel on the screen combines three small and very close but slightly separated RGB light sources. The separate sources of RGB light are indistinguishable at common viewing distances so that our eye–brain color vision system perceives solid color. As noted earlier in this section, *trichromacy* is the term that describes our three channels for color associated with the three cones in our eyes. This principle of trichromacy is further applied to the RGB color model where color is described by the three values of RGB. The concept of defining a color in terms of RGB values is frequently used in color science and is shown in Figure 2.9.

As we have noted, it is possible to create Yellow from Red and Green lights with Blue lights equaling zero. For the example shown in Figure 2.9, Yellow is defined in RGB values as (255, 255, 0). The highest value in this case is 255 and the lowest value is 0. The use of the range of 0–255 to define digital (RGB) color is actually based on a computer memory. Color for a given object is stored in a computer's memory. This computer memory is in the form of on and off switches defined in terms of a long sequence of 0s and 1s. Each switch is called a bit and eight bits form a byte. If there are eight bits (one byte) in a sequence, there are 256 possibilities to configure these switches. This yields a range of numbers between 0 and 255.

FIGURE 2.9   Diagram of the color Yellow in RGB values of Red = 255, Green = 255, and Blue = 0. We define the color of Yellow by using only Red and Green lights with Blue lights equaling zero. (Illustration by Theresa-Marie Rhyne, 2015, using Adobe Color CC [http://color.adobe.com].)

Our human color perception system provides the ability to comprehend the color of objects irrespective of the light source used to illuminate them. For example, we identify the same Yellow color of a banana under bright sunlight, under fluorescent lighting, or candlelight. Even though the surrounding light source might cause more Orange hues or perhaps Green hues to actually reach our eyes, our brain works to correct this situation to keep the Yellow color of the banana constant. This phenomenon is called color constancy. Our brain disregards the continual changes in the wavelengths of light reflected from a surface. This stability in color allows us to categorize color-related properties of objects consistently as we transition through our daily processes of living.

From a precise technical viewpoint, it is actually inappropriate to refer to light as having color [6]. Basically, light is a wave with either a specific wavelength or a mixture of wavelengths. Light has no color itself. Rather, an object that emits or reflects light appears to have color to our eyes. This is due to both our physiological and psychological eye–brain responses to the wavelength. Returning to our Yellow light example, there is light in the range of 577–597 nm that appears Yellow. Although technically imprecise, we will refer to Yellow and other colors of light as we further develop concepts for applying color theory to digital media and visualization in this book. The biology of our color vision is highly complex and still under study even today. We have only provided an overview in regard to how to apply these concepts to creating effective digital media and visualization content. Section 2.8 will discuss color vision deficiencies and how to incorporate this knowledge into digital media design.

2.6 LUMINOSITY

Luminosity is the perceived brightness of a color. Perceived brightness is not necessarily a numerical or measured value associated with a given color model. Figure 2.10 shows the RGB colors in full strength (at a 255 value for each hue) side by side as three individual swatches. The majority of viewers of Figure 2.10 would agree that the Green color is perceptually lighter or more luminous than the Red hue. The Red color is in turn lighter than the Blue hue. Although the numeric values indicate 100% brightness or luminosity (255, respectively), we perceive different tones. If we convert the same image to a Black and White image where the luminosity becomes 0% (000, respectively), we see the brightness of the RGB colors is equal. Differences in perceived luminosity become key parameters in assessing colorimetry data provided by human subjects and the development of the color spaces and systems Color spaces and systems are further discussed in Chapter 3.

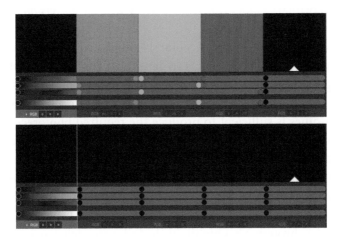

FIGURE 2.10   A study in luminosity where the Red, Green, and Blue (RGB) colors at equal full strength (255 values) are placed side by side. (Illustration created by Theresa-Marie Rhyne, 2015, using Adobe Color CC [http://color.adobe.com].)

2.7 CHROMATICITY

Chromaticity is defined as an objective specification of the quality of a given color irrespective of the given color's luminance. Chromaticity is specified by two independent parameters frequently noted as hue and colorfulness where colorfulness is also defined as saturation, chroma, intensity, or purity depending on the particular color space under discussion [9]. Chapter 3 defines and covers many color spaces that use differing colorfulness parameters. These include spaces: (1) Hue Saturation and Value (HSV); (2) Hue Saturation and Brightness (HSB); (3) the Munsell Color System; (4) the International Commission on Illumination (CIE) 1931 XYZ color space; (5) the CIE LUV, and the CIE LAB color spaces.

2.8 COLOR VISION DEFICIENCIES

As noted previously, color vision is possible due to the cones or photoreceptors in the retina of the eye. In humans, the existence of three types of photopigments where each is sensitive to different parts of the visual spectrum of light provides for a rich color vision. Pigments inside the cones register differing colors that are sent through the optic nerve to the brain. Since the eye and the brain work together to translate light into color, each person sees color differently. For individuals with normal color vision, these differences are slight. However, if the cones lack one or more of the light-sensitive pigments, it is not possible for the eye to view one or more of the RGB primary colors [10]. This is defined as a *color vision deficiency* or as a type of color blindness.

The most common types of color blindness are considered to be hereditary and result from defects in genes that contain instructions for producing the photopigments found in cones [11]. These genes for photopigment production are carried on the X chromosome. Only one of the X chromosomes is sufficient to produce the required photoreceptors for color vision. If these genes are missing or damaged, the probability is higher that a color deficiency will appear in males rather than in females. This is due to males having only one X chromosome and females having two X chromosomes. A color deficiency can also be produced by physical or chemical damage to the eye, optic nerve, or parts of the brain [12]. Sections 2.8.1 through 2.8.4 highlight the following deficiencies: (1) Red–Green; (2) Blue–Yellow; (3) color monochromacy; and (4) rod monochromacy deficiencies.

2.8.1 Red Cone Color Deficiency

The most common form of color vision deficiency is Red–Green. Red–Green hereditary color blindness can be due to following reasons: (1) the limited function or loss of the Red cone (called protan) or (2) the limited function or loss of the Green cone (called deutran) photopigments. Protanomaly and protanopia are Red cone photopigment disorders. With protanomaly, the Red cone is abnormal with Red, Orange, and Yellow hues appearing Greener in tone. Individuals with protanomaly may also note that colors appear duller than individuals with normal color vision. This is considered a mild color deficiency that rarely interferes with daily living and is projected to affect 1% of males. Protanopia, a more severe color deficiency, involves no working red cone cells. Red appears as Black and some shades of Orange, Yellow, and Green appear as Yellow. Protanopia is estimated to affect 1% of the male population. Figure 2.11 depicts a Red cone color deficiency simulation created using the Coblis color blindness simulation tool.

2.8.2 Green Cone Color Deficiency

Deuteranomaly, where the Green cone is abnormal, is the most common form of color deficiency. With deuteranomaly, Yellow and Green appear Redder and it is difficult to differentiate Violet from Blue. This color deficiency affects about 5% of the male population and is considered to be a mild disorder that does not affect daily living. Deuteranopia is the color deficiency with no working Green cone cells. For this case, Red appears as Brownish-Yellow and Green appears as Beige. Deuteranopia affects about 1% of the male population. Figure 2.12 depicts a Green cone color deficiency simulation created using the Coblis color blindness simulation tool.

Normal vision **Protanomaly:** **Protanopia:**
limited loss **severe loss**
of Red cone **of Red cone**

FIGURE 2.11 *Red cone* color deficiency simulation. (Illustration created by Theresa-Marie Rhyne, 2015, using Coblis [http://www.color-blindness.com/coblis-color-blindness-simulator/].)

| Normal vision | Deuteranomaly:
limited loss
of Green cone | Deuteranopia:
severe loss
of Green cone |

FIGURE 2.12 *Green cone* color deficiency simulation. (Illustration created by Theresa-Marie Rhyne, 2015, using Coblis [www.color-blindness.com /coblis-color-blindness-simulator/].)

2.8.3 Blue Cone Color Deficiency

There are also Blue–Yellow color deficiencies where the Blue cone (tritan) photopigments have either limited function or are missing. Blue–Yellow color deficiencies occur less frequently than Red–Green color blindness and can affect males and females equally. With tritanomaly, the functionality of Blue cone cells is limited. Blue appears Greener and it is challenging to differentiate Yellow and Red from Pink. This is an extremely rare color deficiency condition. Tritanopia is the color deficiency associated with a lack of Blue cone cells and is identified as Blue–Yellow color blindness. Blue appears as Green with Yellow appearing as Violet or Light Gray. Tritanopia is an extremely rare color deficiency affecting males and females. Figure 2.13 depicts a Blue cone color deficiency simulation created using the Coblis color blindness simulation tool.

2.8.4 Color Monochromacy and Rod Monochromacy

Additionally, there are two extraordinarily rare forms of color deficiency called color monochromacy and rod monochromacy. Color monochromacy is the result of two of the three photopigments not functioning. As we discussed earlier, the brain needs to compare signals from different cones to produce color vision. So, individuals with Red monochromacy, Green monochromacy, or Blue monochromacy are challenged to distinguish color. Individuals with Blue monochromacy can have additional vision difficulties such as near-sightedness or lack of visual acuity [11]. Rod monochromacy, also called achromatopsia, is a severe form of color blindness where none of the cone cells have functioning pigments. This condition is present at birth and results in seeing the world in Black, White, and Gray tones. Individuals with rod monochromacy tend to be uncomfortable in bright environments since

 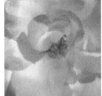 

Normal vision	**Tritanomaly:** **limited loss** **of blue cone**	**Tritanopia:** **severe loss** **of blue cone**

FIGURE 2.13 *Blue cone* color deficiency simulation. (Illustration created by Theresa-Marie Rhyne, 2015, using Coblis [www.color-blindness.com/coblis-color-blindness-simulator/].)

Normal vision	**Blue cone** **monochromacy**	**Rod cone** **monochromacy:** **achromatopsia**

FIGURE 2.14 *Monochromacy* color deficiency simulation. (Illustration created by Theresa-Marie Rhyne, 2015, using Coblis [www.color-blindness.com /coblis-color-blindness-simulator/].)

the rods in the eye respond to dim lighting [11]. As noted earlier, color monochromacy and rod monochromacy are highly rare conditions in the human population. Figure 2.14 depicts a monochromacy cone color deficiency simulation created using the Coblis color blindness simulation tool.

2.9 SIMULATING AND DESIGNING FOR COLOR DEFICIENCIES

There are several online tools that provide assistance in showing what images look like to individuals with color blindness. These simulation tools aid in designing digital media and visualizations to address color deficiencies. Coblis is a freely available color blindness simulation tool. It allows importing a jpeg image and viewing how that image appears under various color deficiency situations. We used Coblis to help us depict color deficiencies shown in Figures 2.11 through 2.14. The tool is available online at www.color-blindness.com/coblis-color-blindness-simulator/. Vischeck is another color blindness simulation tool for checking digital images stored in a jpeg format. Vischeck is available online at: www. vischeck.com. A jpg or jpeg is a frequently used compression format for digital images that was created in 1992. The acronym "jpeg" stands for the Joint Photographic Experts Group (JPEG) who created the digital image format. Detailed information on the jpeg digital image format is available at the JEPG Web site (www.jpeg.org/jpeg).

There are also color scheme suggestion tools that include a color blindness simulation function as part of their color scheme recommendation process. Color Scheme Designer is an example of an online color scheme suggestion tool that has a vision simulation function. The vision simulation addresses the color deficiencies that we outlined previously. Color Scheme Designer is available from Paletton.com at http://paletton.com. The ColorBrewer online tool for color advice in cartography includes a color-blind safe function for its recommended color schemes. The ColorBrewer tool is available at http://colorbrewer2.org. Color Scheme Designer and ColorBrewer are featured in Chapter 5. We have only named a few of the color simulation and suggestion tools that include color vision simulation functions. There are many additional tools available for addressing color deficiency in digital media and visualization design.

We note the following URLs to selected online software tools that address color deficiencies:

Coblis: www.color-blindness.com/coblis-color-blindness-simulator/

Vischeck: www.vischeck.com

Color Scheme Designer: http://paletton.com/

Colorbrewer: http://colorbrewer2.org

2.10 EXAMPLE OF APPLYING COLOR DEFICIENCY STUDIES

In this example, a pie chart or color wheel is created that also represents the primary and secondary colors of the RYB color model. We discussed the RYB color model in Section 1.3 of Chapter 1. These primary colors are Red, Yellow, and Blue, while the secondary colors are Orange,

FIGURE 2.15 Example of applying color deficiency simulation analysis to the Red, Yellow, and Blue primary and secondary color wheel. Individuals with Red–Green (protanopia), Green–Red (deuteranopia), and Blue–Yellow (tritanopia) color deficiencies cannot differentiate the Red, Orange, Yellow, Green, Blue, and Purple colors that a person with normal color vision is able to detect. (Illustration created by Theresa-Marie Rhyne, 2015, using Vischeck [http://www.vischeck .com/vischeck/vischeckImage.php].)

Green, and Purple. A pie chart or color wheel is created with equal distributions of these colors in the clockwise order of Red, Orange, Yellow, Green, Blue, and Purple. These selected colors have similarities to the colors of Newton's rainbow diagram of Figure 1.3 and Newton's color circle of Figure 1.7 discussed in Chapter 1. Next, VisCheck is used, as a color deficiency check, to assess how our color wheel jpeg image would look to individuals with protanopia, deuteranopia, and tritanopia. The results are shown in Figure 2.15.

From our color wheel example, in Figure 2.15, we can determine that individuals with Red–Green (protanopia) or Green–Red (deuteranopia) deficiencies would not be able to easily tell the difference between the colors of Red, Orange, and Green. In addition, the colors of Blue and Purple appear to have different shading values, but do not appear as distinctively different colors for individuals with protanopia or deuteranopia. For individuals with Blue–Yellow (tritanopia) deficiencies, the colors of Yellow, Orange, Red, and Purple appear to have different shading values, but do not appear as distinctively different colors. Individuals with tritanopia also view Green and Blue to be different shades of each other rather than as distinctively different colors. So, if we apply the Red, Orange, Yellow, Green, Blue, and Purple color mapping or color scheme to a data visualization problem, individuals with color deficiencies might not gain the intended insight during the visual analysis process. In Section 2.11, we describe some other challenges in working with this color scheme. This particular color scheme is also called a "rainbow" color map.

FIGURE 2.16   Nonuniform distances between hues in rainbow color maps. (Illustration created by Theresa-Marie Rhyne, 2016.)

2.11 PROBLEMS WITH THE RAINBOW COLOR MAP

Many visualization tools have used the *rainbow*, also called the *Newtonian*, color map, as the default color palette in their visual analysis functions. As shown in Figure 2.16, the distances between Red, Orange, Yellow, Green, Blue, Indigo, and Purple color are not perceptually uniform. When viewing data visualized with a rainbow color scheme, changes or transitions in data can be perceived incorrectly. Rogowitz and Treinish reported these concerns in their 1998 article, "Data Visualization: The End of the Rainbow," while Borland and Taylor highlighted additional issues in a 2007 paper, "Rainbow Color Map (Still) Considered Harmful" [13,14]. Additionally, in 2011, Borkin and her team reported their findings from user studies on the application of various color maps, including the rainbow color map, to medical visualization problems [15]. Their research reported that a perceptually uniform color map resulted in fewer diagnostic errors than the rainbow color map. Many visualization researchers have implemented software solutions to building color maps for addressing these limitations. In 2009, Kenneth Moreland proposed a solution in his paper "Diverging Color Maps for Scientific Visualization" that was incorporated into his *gencolormap* software as well as into the open-source large-scale visualization tool entitled *ParaView* [16]. In 2016, Moreland also published a paper, "Why We Use Bad Color Maps and What You Can Do about It." that provides his practical advice on color map solutions beyond the rainbow color map [17].

2.12 CONCLUDING REMARKS

This chapter provides a general overview of color vision principles, including color deficiencies. Tools are introduced to help analyze how individuals with color deficiencies might view a digital image or visualization. How the use of a rainbow color map in visualizing data can produce perceptual errors in analyzing trends in the data is also discussed. Chapter 3 examines color gamut, color spaces, and color systems and highlights the fundamentals behind the terminology used in online and mobile color applications.

REFERENCES

1. Bruno, T.J. and Svoronos, P.D.N. (2005). *CRC Handbook of Fundamental Spectroscopic Correlation Charts*. Boca Raton, FL: CRC Press.
2. Wandell, B.A. (1995). *The Foundations of Vision*. Sunderland, MA: Sinauer Associates. Available at https://foundationsofvision.stanford.edu/.
3. von Helmholtz, H. (1910). *Hermann von Helmholtz's Treatise on Physiological Optics*. Translated by J.P.C. Southall. New York, NY: The Optical Society of America: Dover Publications. Available at http://poseidon.sunyopt.edu/BackusLab/Helmholtz/.
4. Hering, E. (1878). *Outlines of a Theory of the Light Sense by Ewald Hering*. Translated by L.M. Hurvich and D. Jameson. Cambridge, MA: Harvard University Press.
5. Hurvich, L.M. and Jameson, D. (1957). An opponent-process theory of color vision. *Psychological Review*, 64: 384–404.
6. Gouras, P. (2009). Color Vision, Webvision, University of Utah School of Medicine. Available at http://webvision.med.utah.edu/book/part-vii-color-vision/color-vision/.
7. Bowmaker, J.K. and Dartnall, H.J.A. (1980). Visual pigments of rods and cones in a human retina. *Journal of Physiology*, 298: 501–511.
8. Stone, M. (2003). Color vision. In *A Field Guide to Digital Color*, Canada: A.K. Peters/CRC Press, pp. 43–64.
9. Schanda, J. (2007). *Colorimetry: Understanding the CIE System*. Hoboken, NJ: John Wiley & Sons.
10. Byrne, A. and Hilbert, D.R. (eds.). (1997). *Readings on Color, Volume 2: The Science of Color*. Cambridge, MA: MIT Press.
11. Neitz, J. et al. (2011). Color vision. In L.A. Levin et al. (eds.), *Adler's Physiology of the Eye*, Eleventh Edition. New York, NY: Saunders, pp. 648–654.
12. Hilbert, D.R. and Byrne, A. (2010). How do things look to the color-blind? In J. Cohen and M. Matthen (eds.), *Color Ontology and Color Science*. Cambridge MA: MIT Press, pp. 259–290.
13. Rogowitz, B.E. and Treinish, L.A. (1998). Data visualization: The end of the rainbow. *IEEE Spectrum*, 35(12): 52–59.
14. Borland, D. and Taylor II, R.M. (2007). Rainbow color map (still) considered harmful. *IEEE Computer Graphics and Applications*, 27(2): 14–17.

15. Borkin, M., Gajos, K., Peters, A., et al. (2011). Evaluation of artery visualizations for heart disease diagnosis. *IEEE Transactions on Visualization and Computer Graphics*, 17(2): 2479–2488.
16. Moreland, K. (2009). Diverging color maps for scientific visualization. *ISVC '09 Proceedings of the 5th International Symposium on Advances in Visual Computing*: Part II. Berlin, Springer-Verlag, pp. 92–103.
17. Moreland, K. (2016). Why we use bad color maps and what you can do about it. *HVEI 2016 Proceedings of Human Vision and Electronic Imaging.* Available at http://www.kennethmoreland.com/color-advice/BadColorMaps.pdf.

CHAPTER 3

Defining Color Gamut, Color Spaces, and Color Systems

3.1 COLOR GAMUT

Color gamut is a term used to describe the range of colors a device can reproduce. As indicated in Figure 2.1, the human eye–brain visual system can view a range of colors defined as the visible spectrum. Color imaging devices such as digital cameras, mobile phones, scanners, monitors, and printers have a smaller and narrower range of colors. Almost every device has a different color gamut. Color images on one device such as your mobile phone will look different when printed from your ink jet printer due to the different range of colors reproducible on each of the respective devices. In Chapter 1, we highlighted the Red, Green, and Blue (RGB) display and Cyan, Magenta, Yellow, and Key Black (CMYK) printing color models, showing their complementary relationship in Figure 1.6. In general, the range of colors displayed on an RGB display device or a computer monitor is usually greater than the range of colors that can be produced by a CMYK printer. Converting digital media between devices alters the color gamut of the original source image with some colors being lost in the process. Figure 3.1 shows a comparison between RGB and CMYK color gamut ranges and demonstrates how RGB display colors transfer to CMYK printed colors.

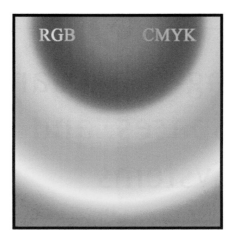

FIGURE 3.1   Comparison of Red, Green, and Blue (RGB) and Cyan, Magenta, Yellow, and Key Black (CMYK) color gamut ranges. This figure shows that the RGB color gamut differs from the CMYK color gamut. As a result digital RGB images often appear altered when printed on a CMYK printer. (Image originally created by Annette Shacklett in 2003 using Adobe Photoshop and is in the public domain by request of the creator, https://commons.wikimedia.org/wiki/File:RGB_CMYK_4.jpg.)

In Chapter 2, we defined the luminosity or perceived brightness of a color. Figure 2.10 shows a comparison between RGB hues at full strength or the highest luminosity. Typically, Reds, Greens, and Blues with high luminosity on an RGB display device are not easily reproduced using only CMYK ink or toner. Defining a color gamut for these respective systems helps us understand the variances in color ranges and determine optimal colors that will transfer effectively between devices. At present, there are no devices that can reproduce the entire visible spectrum of human color vision. Working toward this unrealized goal has resulted in improved color display, scanning and printing technologies.

How do we draw or diagram the color gamut of a device? A common method used is to work with the *x–y chromaticity diagram of the XYZ color space* established in 1931 by the International Commission on Illumination (or *Commission Internationale de l'Eclairage*, CIE). In Chapter 2, we defined chromaticity as an objective specification of the quality of a given color irrespective of the given color's luminance. Figure 3.2 shows the color gamut for a typical computer monitor. The Gray upside-down "U"-shaped region (often called a horseshoe) indicates the range of chromaticities visible to humans, based on the CIE

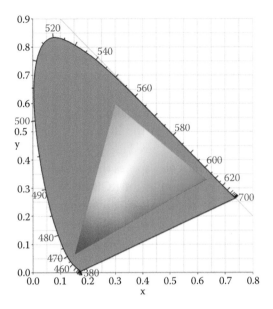

FIGURE 3.2 The color gamut of a typical computer monitor. The Gray upside-down-U or horseshoe shape represents the entire range of colors in the visible spectrum or chromaticity values based on the International Commission on Illumination (CIE) 1931 XYZ color space. (Image originally created by Hankwang and Aboalbliss in 2006 using Adobe Photoshop and is in the public domain by request of the creators, https://commons.wikimedia.org /wiki/File:CIExy1931_srgb_gamut.png.)

1931 chromaticity diagram. The colored triangle inside the *horseshoe* represents the color gamut available to some particular device. The corners of the triangle show the primary colors of this gamut, with Red being the right point of the triangle, Green being the top point of the triangle, and Blue being the left point of the triangle. In Section 3.5, we describe the development of the CIE *x–y* chromaticity diagram in further detail. This is the grayed-out portion of Figure 3.2, including the rainbow-color triangle. For a general overview of color gamut and color models, we refer you to Ibraheem et al. [1].

3.2 COLOR SPACES

Figure 3.2 also shows the *color space* of a typical computer monitor. For this situation, our color space is the combination of the RGB color model and the color gamut of the given typical computer monitor. This relationship is summarized as follows: RGB Color Model + Color Gamut = Color Space. A color space can be an arbitrary color system or structured mathematically. The Pantone matching system (PMS) is an example of an arbitrary color system based on color swatches and corresponding assigned names. We will discuss the *PMS* later in Section 3.10 of this chapter. As we noted in Chapter 2, a color model with a mathematical structure can be represented as tuples of numbers. For the RGB color model, three numbers represent the RGB values as we showed for Yellow (255, 255, 000) in Figure 2.9. There are several specific color spaces that are based on the RGB color model. A complete specification of an RGB color space also includes a White point chromaticity value and a *gamma correction curve*. Refer to Ibraheem et al. [1], and Schanda [2] for further details on complete specifications of the RGB color space, as this is beyond the scope of our efforts. In Figure 3.2, we see a White point inside the triangle where the colors converge. Susstrunk, Buckely, and Swen in their 1999 paper "Standard RGB Color Spaces" describe the specifications and usage of standard RGB color spaces. For a more detailed discussion of the derivation and mathematical structure of RGB color spaces, see Reference [3].

3.3 COMMONLY APPLIED RGB COLOR SPACES

The most commonly applied RGB color spaces in digital media and visualization are sRGB, Adobe RGB, and ProPhoto RGB. Hewlett-Packard Company and Microsoft Corporation cooperatively created and then proposed sRGB as a standard, in 1996, to approximate the color gamut of the most common computer display devices. Since sRGB effectively serves as a best guess for how the majority of monitors, mobile phones, and digital cameras produce color, it has become the standard color space for displaying images on the Internet. As a result, many software applications and Web specifications are designed around the sRGB specification. The sRGB color gamut includes approximately 35% of the visible colors specified in the 1931 CIE chromaticity diagram.

Adobe RGB was developed and published in 1998 by Adobe Systems, Inc., to encompass the majority of colors supported by CMYK printers using only RGB primary colors on display devices. The Adobe RGB color space is targeted at providing fewer challenges in transferring colors from RGB displays to CMYK printing output devices. The Adobe RGB color gamut includes approximately 50% of the visible colors specified in the 1931 CIE chromaticity diagram. Adobe RGB supports richer Cyan and Green hues than sRGB.

Kodak began development on ProPhoto RGB in the late 1990s with the specification becoming available in the early 2000s. The intent was to offer a very large gamut, beyond that available with sRGB, designed for use with photographic output. ProPhoto RGB encompasses about 79% of the colors specified in the 1931 chromaticity diagram. The recognized downside of ProPhoto RGB is that approximately 13% of the colors in ProPhoto RGB color space do not exist and are thus *imaginary* colors. As a result, converting a ProPhoto RGB image to sRGB, Adobe RGB, or CMYK formats can result in unexpected and undesired colors. Many digital photographers prefer to work in ProPhoto RGB in order to preserve the color gamut of their original digital images. Figure 3.3 shows the color gamut map of the color spaces we have described here. The 2200 Matt Paper notation in Figure 3.3 refers to the CMYK color space of an Epson 220 color ink jet printer. References [4,5] provide more details about these commonly applied RGB color spaces.

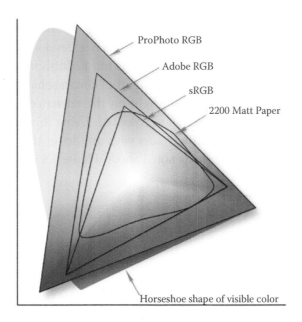

FIGURE 3.3 The gamut map of commonly applied RGB Color Spaces. This figure compares the sRGB, Adobe RGB, and ProPhoto RGB color spaces using the entire range of colors in the visible spectrum or chromaticity values based on the CIE 1931 XYZ color space. The CMYK color space is also depicted as 2200 Matt Paper or the printed output from an Epson 2200 color ink jet printer. (Image created by Jeff Schewe in May 2007 and is in the public domain by request of the creator, https://commons.wikimedia.org/wiki/File:Colorspace.png.)

3.4 COLORIMETRY

The science of color measurement and matching is called *colorimetry*. As we discussed in our definition of metamerism in Section 2.5, when we observe a colored object, our visual system has no way of knowing from its appearance the spectral composition of the physical stimulus. Our brain does not distinguish a Yellow light from an equal combination of Red and Green lights with zero Blue light. Colorimetry provides a system of color measurement and specification based on the concept of equivalent-appearing stimuli. Colorimetry data are gathered from the empirical studies of colors matching by humans. The task of each human subject is to use the three primary lights of RGB to match a designated *reference* color. When a match is established, the reference color can then be defined in terms of the amount of the respective RGB lights required to produce the equivalent reference color. The observer is developing a set of *tristimulus* values. Figure 3.4 shows a schematic diagram of colorimetry color matching by observers.

With colorimetry work, there is the challenge of how to handle reference colors that cannot be matched. The practice developed is to apply a *negative light*. If the blend of RGB lights is too Reddish for color matching even though no Red light is shining, the human subject is permitted to shine some of the Red primary light on the reference color to make the desired match. These results are recorded. Using this approach, it is possible to match all remaining colors with any set of the RGB distinct colors using the *negative light* as noted above. Figure 3.5 depicts the color

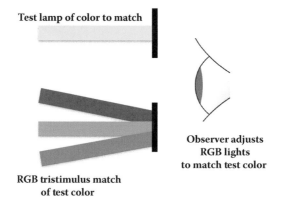

Test lamp of color to match

Observer adjusts
RGB lights
to match test color

RGB tristimulus match
of test color

FIGURE 3.4 Diagram of a colorimetry experiment where an observer adjusts a set of RGB lights to match a test lamp of color. (Illustration by Theresa-Marie Rhyne, 2015.)

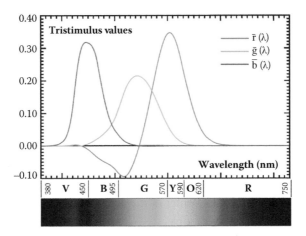

FIGURE 3.5 Color matching functions developed for CIE 1931 RGB colorimetry efforts. (Diagram created by Marco Polo in November 2007 and is in the public domain by request of the creator, https://commons.wikimedia.org/wiki /File:CIE1931_RGBCMF.svg. Color spectrum image created by Gringer in 2008 and is in the public domain by request of the creator, https://commons.wikimedia. org/wiki/File:Linear_visible_spectrum.svg.)

matching functions used in colorimetry tests associated with the CIE 1931 RGB color space.

We will further discuss these concepts in the next section on CIE *XYZ* and *xyY* Color Spaces. A robust multiauthored publication on colorimetry entitled *Colorimetry: Understanding the CIE System* was edited by Janos Schanda in 2007 [2]. Maureen Stone provides a more generic but a detailed overview of colorimetry experiments in the first chapter (Color Vision) of her 2003 book titled *A Field Guide to Digital Color* [6].

3.5 THE CIE *XYZ* COLOR SPACE AND THE CIE *X–Y* CHROMATICITY DIAGRAM

The CIE was founded in 1913 to serve as an autonomous international board for the exchange of information and to set standards on items related to lighting. As part of this mission, CIE has a technical committee entitled *Vision and Colour* that has served as a leading force in colorimetry since its first meeting to set standards in 1931. The CIE 1931 color space was developed to be independent of devices or other means of emission or reproduction of color. The standard was based on colorimetry experiments, conducted by William David Wright and John Guild in the 1920s, about how humans perceive color. Wright published his results in 1929, while Guild, independently, published his results in 1931. As shown in Figure 3.4, the human subjects (or observers) in these colorimetry experiments developed tristimulus values by visually matching a test color against the RGB primary colors. Figure 3.5 shows the color matching functions used in developing CIE RGB color space. Due to the distribution of cones in our eyes, tristimulus values are dependent on an observer's field of view. The CIE established a color mapping function called *the standard (colorimetric) observer* to remove this variable. The *CIE 1931 Standard Observer* (also called the CIE 1931 2° Standard Observer) is based on the assumption that color-sensitive cones are located within 2° of the arc of the fovea inside the retina of the eye. As stated in Section 2.2, the fovea is at the center of the retina in our eyes.

CIE considered the use of direct RGB data from the human subject colorimetry studies to be undesirable for establishing a standardized color space. This concern pertained to study results that permitted negative RGB values as shown in Figure 3.5. Instead, a mathematical formula was developed to convert the RGB data to a system of only positive integers. These reformulated values were noted as *XYZ*. The resulting *XYZ* numbers approximate but do not directly correspond to the RGB values of the Wright and Guild colorimetry studies. Figure 3.6 depicts the resulting

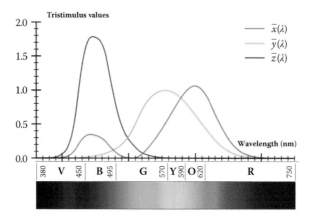

FIGURE 3.6 Diagram of the CIE standard observer functions that resulted from converting the original CIE RGB data into the CIE XYZ system of only positive integers. (Plot created by Acdx in March 2009 and can be copied, distributed, and modified under the GNU Free Documentation License, https://commons.wikimedia.org/wiki/File:CIE_1931_XYZ_Color_Matching _Functions.svg. Color spectrum image created by Gringer in 2008 and is in the public domain by request of the creator, https://commons.wikimedia.org/wiki /File:Linear_visible_spectrum.svg.)

CIE *XYZ* tristimulus values that are also called the CIE standard observer matching functions.

CIE also derived a two-dimensional equivalent to the CIE *XYZ* color space called the *CIE x–y chromaticity diagram*. This is the horseshoe-shaped diagram that we have discussed in Sections 3.1 and 3.3. CIE established a new set of chromacity coordinates called *x*, *y*, and *z* exhibiting the property that *x* + *y* + *z* = 1. The coordinate *z* is not displayed in the CIE *x–y* chromaticity diagram, but can be derived from the *x* + *y* + *z* = 1 relationship. The two-dimensional visualization is a result of developing a chart with *x* and *y* as its axes to plot points that indicate chromaticity. In working with the CIE *XYZ* color space, the tristimulus values are always indicated in upper case as *X*, *Y*, and *Z* and the chromaticity coordinates are always noted in lower case as *x*, *y*, and *z*. We show this visualization of the CIE *x–y* chromaticity diagram in Figure 3.7.

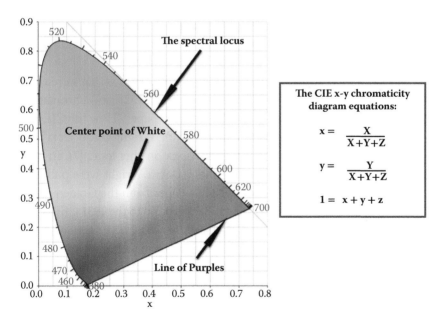

FIGURE 3.7   CIE x–y chromaticity diagram that results from the CIE XYZ color space tristimulus value being converted into chromaticity coordinates of *x*, *y*, and *z* according to the equations noted. The *z* values do not appear but can be calculated due to the 1 = *x* + *y* + *z* equation. (Image created by PAR in June 2005 and is in the public domain by request of the creator, https://en.wikipedia.org/wiki/File:CIExy1931.png#/media/File:CIExy1931.png. Text annotations and additions of equations provided by Theresa-Marie Rhyne, 2015.)

Plotting the x and y values of spectral colors ranging from 400 to 700 nm on the x–y chromaticity diagram results in a horseshoe-shaped curve that we introduced in Section 3.1. The edge line of this horseshoe-shaped diagram is called *The Spectral Locus*. The spectral locus represents pure monochromatic light measured by wavelength in nanometers. These are the most saturated colors of the horseshoe. Notice the correspondence between the spectral locus values in Figure 3.7 with the visible light spectrum in Figure 2.1. The nonspectral Magenta or Purple-Red mixtures fall along the straight line joining the 400-nm point to the 700-nm point of the horseshoe. This line is often termed the *Line of Purples*. The colors of the Line of Purples are also fully saturated and are made by mixing Red and Blue colors. All visible colors fall within the resulting closed horseshoe curve. Pale and unsaturated colors lie nearer the center of the diagram. The central point of $x = 1/3$ and $y = 1/3$ is defined as the achromatic point where visually perceived *White* is located. If we define two colors in the chromaticity diagram as individual end points and place a line between them, the colors along the resulting line are produced via combinations of the two color end points. The line of Purples is one demonstration of this characteristic.

There are many principles and mathematical functions that were established in developing the CIE *XYZ* color space and the CIE *x*–*y* chromaticity diagram. In 1997, Fairman et al. published their paper "How the CIE 1931 Color-Matching Functions Were Derived from Wright-Guild Data" that provides one of the more detailed discussions on this topic [7]. In 2007, the reflections and perspectives of William David Wright were published in a discussion entitled "Professor Wright's Paper from the Golden Jubilee Book: The Historical and Experimental Background to the 1931 CIE System of Colorimetry," in *Colorimetry: Understanding the CIE System*, edited by Janos Schanda [8]. We refer you to these papers for further discussion on the development of the CIE 1931 system for colorimetry. One of the shortcomings of the CIE *x*–*y* chromaticity diagram is that colors of equal amounts of difference appear further apart in the Green region of the visualization than they do in the Red or Violet part. It is frequently noted that Green takes up a disproportionally large fraction of the horseshoe shape compared to the other colors. To address this issue of nonuniform scaling, CIE adopted two uniform diagrams, CIE LUV and CIE LAB, as specifications in 1976. We will highlight CIE LUV and CIE LAB in the next sections of this chapter. Despite this problem of nonuniform scaling, the CIE *x*–*y* chromaticity visualization remains the most common chromaticity diagram in use.

3.6 CIE LUV AND CIE LAB

In 1942, David Lewis MacAdam published his research in the *Journal of the Optical Society of America* that noted the nonuniform scaling of the CIE *x–y* chromaticity visualization [9]. This research showed that the physical distance of two colors on the CIE *x–y* chromaticity diagram may not be equivalent to their perceptual *distance*. To correct this limitation, a number of uniform chromaticity scale (UCS) solutions were proposed. The UCS solutions used mathematical relationships to transform the *XYZ* values or the *x* and *y* coordinates to a new set of values that created a more nearly perceptually uniform two-dimensional color space. Additionally, the Y lightness scale was replaced with a new scale called L^* that was approximately uniformly spaced and more indicative of actual visual differences. In 1976, CIE adopted two color spaces that more effectively showed uniform color spacing in their values. These are CIE LUV and CIE LAB, with the L^* lightness scale being used in both of these color spaces. The CIE LUV color space was designed specifically for emissive colors that correspond to images captured by a camera or created by computer graphics rendering programs. As a result, CIE LUV is used in the display industry. The CIE LAB color space was developed to characterize color surfaces and dyes. CIE LAB is used widely in the color imaging and printing industries. We highlight aspects of CIE LUV and CIE LAB below.

For the mathematical relationships of UCS solutions as well as further technical information on CIE LUV and CIE LAB, we refer you to the *Digital Color Imaging Handbook*, edited by Sharma and Bala [10,11].

3.6.1 CIE LUV

As noted earlier, CIE LUV is a transformation of the CIE *XYZ* color that represents an attempt to achieve a greater correspondence between physical distance on the graph and perceptual uniformity. CIE LUV is widely used in computer graphics applications. In 1960, CIE adopted a 1960 chromaticity diagram to address the nonuniform scaling, called the 1960 CIE *u, v* chromaticity diagram. However, the *u, v* approach was found to be perceptually unsatisfactory. As a consequence, in 1975, CIE proposed new *u′* and *v′* values. The new scaling thus became $u' = u$ and $v' = 1.5v$. The revised diagram was adopted as the 1976 CIE *u′–v′* diagram. For further details see [11]. Figure 3.8 shows the 1976 CIE *u′–v′* chromaticity diagram with the transformation equations.

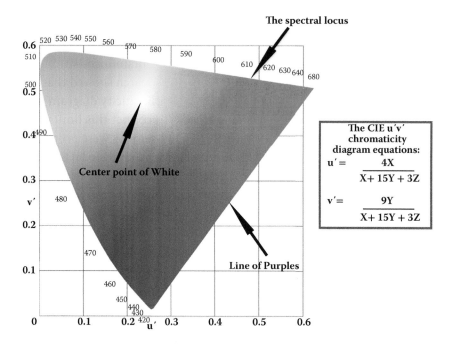

FIGURE 3.8 The 1976 CIE $u'-v'$ chromaticity diagram associated with the CIE LUV color space. (Image created by Adoniscik in March 2008 and is in the public domain by request of the creator, https://en.wikipedia.org/wiki/CIELUV#/media/File:CIE_1976_UCS.png. Text annotations and additions of equations provided by Theresa-Marie Rhyne, 2015.)

The development of UCS solutions to address perceptual uniformity alters the resulting CIE chromaticity visualization. As a result, the Blue-Red portions are elongated and the achromatic White point is relocated in order to ensure a greater correspondence between physical and perceptual distances. The spectral locus is shortened and the Line of Purples is also altered. Figure 3.8 shows these changes that result in the 1976 CIE $u'-v'$ chromaticity diagram [12,13].

3.6.2 CIE LAB

CIE LAB is the second of the two systems that CIE adopted in 1976 to address perceptual uniformity. CIE LAB is a *three-dimensional opponent* color space that accurately represents perceptual distances between different colors. As we mentioned in Section 2.4, Ewald Hering developed the opponent color theory concept in 1878. Opponent theory explains aspects of color vision processing at the neural level when images are transferred from the eye to the brain via the optic nerve. In the brain, retinal color stimuli become translated into distinctions between the following: (1) light and dark (White to Black), (2) Red and Green, and (3) Yellow and Blue. CIE LAB indicates that in these three components one axis (L^*) plots the lightness or luminance from White to Black, a second axis (a^*) plots values between Red and Green, and a third axis (b^*) plots values between Yellow and Blue. These color axes are determined by the concept that a given color cannot simultaneously be Red and Green, or Yellow and Blue, because these colors are in opposition. On the a^* axis, positive values represent amounts of Red, while negative values represent amounts of Green. On the b^* axis, positive values represent amounts of Yellow, whereas negative values represent amounts of Blue. Individual colors are referenced according to their corresponding positions on all three axes. Figure 3.9 shows our three-dimensional representation of CIE $L^*a^*b^*$ color space.

CIE $L^*a^*b^*$ is a device-independent color space that includes all perceivable colors and its gamut exceeds those of the RGB and CMYK color models. This allows CIE $L^*a^*b^*$ to serve as an intermediary color space where values from a particular gamut are re-encoded as CIE $L^*a^*b^*$ values and other devices can convert the resulting CIE $L^*a^*b^*$ values into their own specific color gamut. CIE $L^*a^*b^*$ is a useful framework for linking digital media to color printing technology and provides a color space for painters to better understand the challenges of mixing differently colored

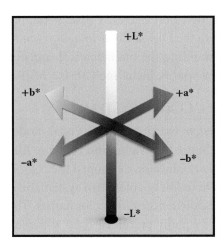

FIGURE 3.9 Three-dimensional representation of the components of the 1976 CIE LAB color space. (Illustration by Theresa-Marie Rhyne, 2015.)

pigments. Many color evaluation tools refer to CIE LAB as "Lab". As we begin to discuss online and mobile tools for color analysis and suggestion, please note that Lab refers to CIE LAB.

The CIE LAB color space is based on efforts that date back to the 1940s. In 1942, Elliott Quincy Adams published "X-Z Planes in the 1931 I.C.I. System of Colorimetry," which describes two color spaces that were precursors to the 1976 CIE LAB and CIE LUV color spaces [14]. In 1944, Dorothy Nickerson and her assistant, K.F. Stultz, built upon Adams' work to develop a color difference formula that in a modified form would eventually become the CIE LAB color space and difference formula [15]. This color difference relationship became known as the Adams-Nickerson-Stultz formula. The 1943 *renotations* and other fundamental aspects of the Munsell color system, covered in the next section, were reviewed as a part of the process of developing the 1976 CIE LAB specification.

Also in the late 1940s, Richard Hunter independently began work on the Hunter Lab color space that evolved through the 1950s and 1960s. In 1966, Hunter released his formulas for converting CIE *XYZ* values to Hunter L, a, b coordinates as Hunter Lab Application Notes [16,17]. The Hunter Lab color space was also a precursor to CIE LAB. The 2012 Hunter Lab Application Note highlights some of the differences between Hunter L, a, b and CIE *L**, *a**, *b** [18].

The CIE LAB specification resulted from fusing these prior contributions. The (*) representations denote mathematical transformations that resulted in creating the final CIE *L**a*b* color space. As we have noted previously under Section 3.6.1 CIE LUV discussion, "Color fundamentals for digital imaging" in the *Digital Color Imaging Handbook* is an excellent reference for understanding the mathematical transformations and relationships of CIE color spaces, including CIE *L**a*b* [10].

3.7 THE MUNSELL COLOR SYSTEM

The *Munsell color system* is a three-dimensional model that defines color as having three attributes: hue, value, and chroma. Albert H. Munsell, an American artist and art educator, developed the color order system in the 1890s to establish a notation of color with systematic order that obviated the need for what he called *misleading* color names. The system is built on the representation of equally perceived color differences as a branching geometry called a *color tree*. The Munsell color order system has served as the basis for a variety of government and industry specifications. These include the U.S. Department of Agriculture's soil conservation and food industry specifications, the American National Standards Institute's color specifications, the National Electrical Manufacturers Association color specifications, and many more. The Munsell color system is also fundamental to many color specifications that followed it, such as CIE LAB. The Munsell color system remains as one of the most popular and internationally used color order systems to this day. It is recognized by the American National Standards Institute (ANSI z138.2), the Japanese Industrial Standard for Color (JIS Z872), the German Standard Color System (DIN 6161), and as a basis for several British national standards. Because of its influence, we discuss it in greater detail below [19].

3.7.1 Evolution of the Munsell Color Order System

Munsell initially conceived of a color sphere as the basis for his system. In 1898, he began a study of the color sensitivities of the human visual system using his own devised experimental tools. From these observations, Munsell came to the conclusion that color space is not naturally geometrically regular. Munsell abandoned the color sphere concept and proposed a three-dimensional color tree model for his color system. The uneven color tree branches are based on equally perceived color differences. Figure 3.10

The color sphere: initially proposed in Munsell's 1905 *Color Notation* publication.

The color tree, as it appeared in the Munsell and Celand 1921 *Grammar of Color* publication.

FIGURE 3.10 Evolution of the Munsell framework. (Illustration combines elements from Munsell, A.H., *A Color Notation*, G.H. Ellis Company, Boston, MA, 1905, plate 1; and Cleland, T.M., et al., *A Grammar of Color: Arrangements of Strathmore Papers in a Variety of Printed Color Combinations According to the Munsell Color System*, Strathmore Paper Co., Mittineague, MA, 1921, p. 18, public domain.)

shows the evolution of Munsell's model for his color order system from a three-dimensional color sphere to a three-dimensional color tree.

In 1905, in his book entitled *A Color Notation,* Munsell described his color theory. In 1915, the *Atlas of the Munsell Color System* book provided 15 charts that illustrated colored specimens for a range of values and chromas of the 10 fundamental hues of the color system. In 1921, after Munsell's death in 1918, *A Grammar of Color: Arrangements of Strathmore Papers in a Variety of Printed Color Combinations According to The Munsell Color System* was published that included an introduction by Munsell along with explanatory text and diagrams applying the system prepared by Thomas Maitland (T.M.) Cleland [20–22].

In 1917, shortly before his death, Munsell founded the Munsell Color Company as a business vehicle for producing color standards. After Munsell's death, his son, Alexander Ector Orr Munsell, built on the elder Munsell's work. The 1929 edition of *The Munsell Book of Color,* with improved color scales, displayed 20 hues. In 1943, using the CIE 1931 standard observer functions (discussed in Section 3.4), a subcommittee of the Optical Society of America recommended *renotations* to the Munsell color system. These renotations were adopted and provided a convenient method for converting standardized color measurement data to the Munsell color system. Additional revisions resulted in the adoption of the Munsell color system as a basis for colorimetry specifications used by those U.S. government agencies previously mentioned. In the early 1950s, the number of hues of in *The Munsell Book of Color* expanded from 20 to 40 hues. Improvements to the Munsell Color Order System have evolved over time. For further reading on the history of the Munsell color system, we refer you to Dorothy Nickerson's 1976 three-part discussion on the system's history [23–25]. The company continues today as a part of X-Rite Inc., a manufacturer of color measurement and color management solutions; see www.munsell.com. More information on the latest versions of *The Munsell Book of Color* are available on this web site. Figure 3.11 provides a combined illustration of the hue, value, and chroma attributes of the Munsell color system from the 1921 book.

3.7.2 Geometry of the Munsell Color Order System

As Figure 3.11 shows, Munsell developed his system as an orb. Around the equator runs a band of colors that defines the *hue* attribute. The axis of the orb encompasses a scale of neutral Gray values with White at the top of the pole and Black at the bottom of the pole. This axis defines the

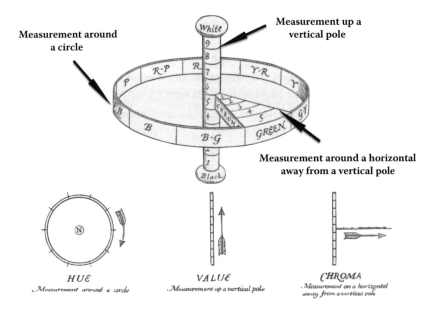

FIGURE 3.11   Combined illustration of the hue, value, and chroma attributes of the three-dimensional Munsell color order system. (From Cleland, T.M. et al., *A Grammar of Color: Arrangements of Strathmore Papers in a Variety of Printed Color Combinations According to the Munsell Color System*, Strathmore Paper Co., Mittineague, MA, 1921, public domain. Illustration combines elements from pages 13 and 16 in the above-cited book. Text annotations added by Theresa-Marie Rhyne, 2015.)

value attribute. Extending horizontally from the axis at each Gray value is a gradation of color moving from neutral Gray at the center of the orb to full saturation at the outer ring. This horizontal progression defines *chroma*. Munsell established numerical scales with visually uniform steps for each of the three attributes. We discuss these attributes in further detail below.

3.7.2.1 Hue
The Munsell color order system defines hue attributes as actual colors and establishes five principle hues. These principle hues are Red (R), Yellow (Y), Green (G), Blue (B), and Purple (P) and are equally spaced in a clockwise order around a color circle or wheel. These principle hues are separated by five intermediate or mixture colors. The intermediate hues are defined as Yellow Red (YR), Green Yellow (GY), Blue Green (BG), Purple Blue (PB), and Red Purple (RP). The color wheel is measured by 100 compass points

resulting in 100 steps on the hue circle. Each of the primary and interme-diate colors is allocated a range of 10° on the color circle and is located at the mid-point of this segment. In the Munsell notation, primary Yellow is identified as 5Y and is at the mid point of its segment. A value of 2.5Y indicates Yellow progressing toward Yellow Red with 7.5Y transitioning toward Green Yellow. A value of 10Y is the end point of the Yellow seg-ment, positioned equally between the primary Yellow (5Y) and intermedi-ate Green Yellow (5GY). This notation concept results in 40 standard hue circle divisions. In the Munsell notation, Orange is defined as Yellow Red. Figure 3.12 shows the Munsell hue circle or color wheel as we described above.

Two colors on opposite sides of the hue wheel are called complementary colors. For 5Y (Yellow), the complementary color in the Munsell notation would be 5PB (Purple Blue). Combining 5Y with 5PB results in the 5N neu-tral Gray color at the center of the Munsell hue wheel shown in Figure 3.12. The Munsell color notation system is designed so that each color has a logical relationship to all other colors. This is called color harmony. In Chapter 4, we will discuss color harmony concepts in further detail.

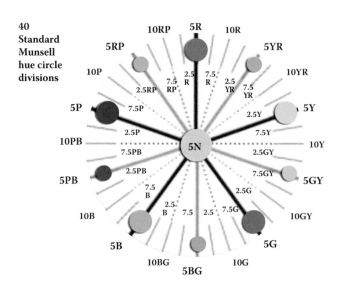

FIGURE 3.12   The Munsell hue wheel divided into 40 circle divisions. (Illustration by Theresa-Marie Rhyne, 2015; adapted from American Society of Testing Materials, ASTM D1535: Specifying Color by the Munsell System, 1968, https:// archive.org/details/gov.law.astm.d1535.1968.)

3.7.2.2 Value

The value of a color refers to how light or dark a given hue is. In the Munsell color order system, the scale of value ranges from 0 for pure Black to 10 for pure White along a vertical axis as shown previously in Figure 3.11. Each step is divided into decimal increments and results in a 100 step lightness scale. Black, White, and the Grays between them are defined as having no hue and are called *neutral colors*. The notation N is used to indicate the Gray value at any point on the vertical axis. Colors that have a hue, as noted in our description of the hue attribute above, are called *chromatic colors*. The value scale is applied to chromatic and neutral colors. The value attribute of the Munsell color order system is considered the backbone or *trunk* of the color tree as shown in Figure 3.11. The hue circle or color wheel resides at 5N or the middle level of the value attribute as noted in Figure 3.12. The value of a specific hue is noted with the value at the end of the hue designation. As an example, 5Y 4/ indicates a middle Yellow at the value level of 4. The value scale is defined as perceptual or visual. It is based on how humans see differences in relative light and is not based on a set of mathematical values from a light source. Munsell originally developed the original value scale based on human subjects' perceptual judgments of mixtures of White and Black paints. In Munsell's original publications, the value attribute ranged from 1 for pure Black to 9 for pure White as Figure 3.11 indicates. The scale range was later changed to be 0 for pure Black and 10 for pure White as we indicated at the start of this discussion on value.

3.7.2.3 Chroma

Chroma measures the weakness or the strength of a color. It represents the purity of a color in regard to saturation. A low chroma value contains more Gray or pastel tones. A high chroma value is highly saturated or more vivid in tone. As Figure 3.11 indicates, the chrome axis extends from the value axis at a right angle. Chroma is not uniform across the color space otherwise we would have the color sphere that Munsell initially proposed and we previously noted in Figure 3.10. Different hues of the Munsell color space can achieve full or saturated chroma at varying locations in the color space [26,27].

In Figure 3.13, as an example, we examine the 5R (Red) hue and compare its chroma scale with its complement, the 5BG (Blue Green) at the middle value (5N). In Munsell notation, the Red hue is noted as (5R 5/) and Blue Green hue is noted as (5BG 5/). The chroma scale starts at zero

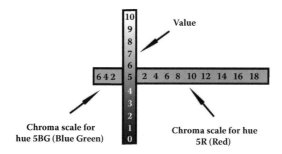

FIGURE 3.13 Differences in chroma scales for two hues of equal value in the Munsell color system. We compare the 5R (Red) hue with its 5BG (Blue Green) complement at the 5N middle value of the Munsell color system. (Illustration by Theresa-Marie Rhyne, 2015.)

for neutral colors and does not have an end. Examining Figure 3.13 indicates that 5R 5/ (Red) has a chroma scale of 18 while 5BG 5/ (Blue Green) has a chroma scale of 6. In the Munsell color notation, this fully saturated Red is noted as (5R 5/18) while the fully saturated Blue Green is noted as (5BG 5/6). So, Red is considered three times as strong as Blue Green in the middle value (5N) location. Chroma paths can change at different steps on the value scale. In the Munsell color space, Reds, Blues, and Purples attain full saturation at mid levels (5/-) of the value scale and are stronger hues with higher chroma values at full saturation. Yellows and Greens reach full saturation at high value levels of (7/-) or (8/-) and are weaker hues with full chroma saturation near the neutral axis. Figure 3.14 shows fully saturated Red (5R 5/18) and fully saturated Yellow (5Y 8/10), each located at different value steps, to illustrate this concept. For more details about particular aspects of the Munsell color order system, see References [28–32].

As highlighted earlier, these differences in chroma values prevent the three-dimensional shape of the Munsell color space from being a symmetrical sphere, and Munsell defined the highly asymmetrical shape as a color tree, previously shown in Figure 3.10. The two-dimensional plots of value and chroma for a given hue depict the branches on the color tree.

3.7.3 Munsell Color Scales and Digital Media

The Munsell color order system dates back to the late nineteenth century, before the development of digital media. Even today, Munsell colors are standardized as carefully prepared paint chips or color samples that are presented as separate pages in a reference catalog entitled *The Munsell Book of Color*. Individual pages of the color atlas include color

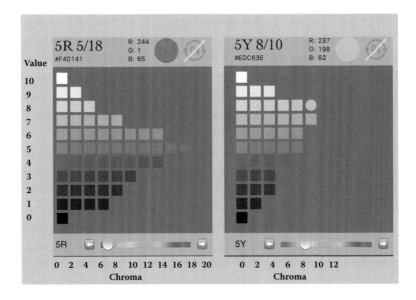

FIGURE 3.14   Comparison of saturated Red (5R 5/18) and saturated Yellow (5Y 8/10) in the Munsell Color Space. Image created using the freely available Munsell DG app by Silicon Goblin Technologies (https://itunes.apple.com/us/developer /silicon-goblin-technologies/id508670615). (Illustration created by Theresa-Marie Rhyne, 2015 using the Munsell DG app by Silicon Goblin Technologies.)

samples of a single hue arranged according to a two-dimensional grid of value on the vertical axis and chroma on the horizontal axis. These are sometimes referred to as color scales. Colors are determined by placing the color specimen against the atlas samples until a color match is found. Such visual evaluations are considered accurate only if the comparison specimens are as large as the atlas color samples and if a Gray background under the same daylight or incandescent illumination is consistently used for assessments. As indicated earlier, *The Munsell Book of Color* is available from the Munsell Color Company (www.munsell.com).

Digital color solutions and libraries have also been developed from *The Munsell Book of Color* and other standards based on the Munsell color space. ASTM International, an international standards organization that develops and publishes voluntary consensus technical standards, has made available conversion formulas and lookup tables to produce a Munsell equivalent for the CIE *XYZ* specification. These conversion formulas also facilitate translation of the Munsell color space to and from any other modern color system able to convert to CIE standards. We covered the CIE *XYZ* color space in Section 3.5. The Munsell Color Science Laboratory provides digital Munsell hue, value, and chroma and CIE *x*, *y*, and *Y* data for free use. The Munsell Color Science Laboratory is located at the Rochester Institute of Technology with a Web site at http://www.cis.rit.edu/research/mcsl2/online/munsell.php [33]. There are many software applications that are available for creating digital versions of the atlas pages in *The Munsell Book of Color.* WallkillColor (www.wallkillcolor.com) is one example [34].

Several applications are available for mobile phones that provide a digital version of *The Munsell Book of Color*, converted to sRGB color space for display. We discussed the sRGB color space in Section 3.3. Some of these mobile apps can be found on the GooglePlay and iTunes online stores. To develop the images previously shown in Figure 3.14, we used the free Munsell DG app for the iPhone from Silicon Goblin Technologies (https://itunes.apple.com/us/app/munselldg/id515717868?mt=8). The Munsell DG app provides corresponding RGB and Web color hex codes for the Munsell hues shown. It is important to remember that these codes result from the color space conversions we described above and are approximate [35].

Although physical comparison of color specimens to carefully prepared paint chips or color samples can be considered out of date with regard to digital media, it turns out to be one of the more accurate methods of color matching. This is because any digital color library cannot depict color specimens consistently or accurately due to the color gamut constraints of RGB display devices. We defined and highlighted color gamut in Section 3.1.

3.8 HUE, SATURATION, AND VALUE (HSV) AND HUE, SATURATION, AND LIGHTNESS (HSL) COLOR SPACES

The *Hue, Saturation, and Value* (HSV) and *Hue, Saturation, and Lightness* (HSL) color spaces are three-dimensional cylindrical-coordinate representations of the RGB color model. These models were established to create intuitively easier and more perceptually relevant mixing of additive RGB color lights. Members of the computer graphics community developed HSV, frequently referred to as HSB where B stands for brightness, and HSL, often referred to as HLS, in the 1970s to support computer graphics applications. Today, HSV and HSL color spaces are frequently used in digital color selection and image editing software. We highlight the history, geometric aspects, and the application of HSV and HSL below.

3.8.1 The Challenge of Mixing RGB Lights

As discussed in Section 3.1, combining RGB lights produces the color gamut or color range of display devices. The process of mixing RGB lights to produce various colors is not always intuitive or perceptually relevant. Figure 3.15 shows how a colorful Yellow of Red = 255, Green = 224, and Blue = 97 can be reduced to what perceptually appears to be half of its colorfulness with a less-saturated Yellow of R = 214, Green = 193, and Blue = 118. This results in a decrease in Red by 41, a decrease in Green by 31, and an increase in Blue by 21 as Figure 3.15 illustrates. This RGB reduction methodology is not necessarily intuitive or logical in our efforts to select digital color combinations.

HSV and HSL color spaces were developed to accommodate more traditional and intuitive ways of mixing colors such as those used by painters for centuries with the Red, Yellow, and Blue (RYB) painters color space. Painters mix bright and colorful pigments with White to achieve a *tint*, with Gray to achieve a *tone,* or with Black to achieve a *shade*. In Figure 3.15, these options were not easily available to us when working with the RGB sliders. HSV and HSL color spaces were also designed to address human vision factors such as those we discussed in Chapter 2 and follow color organization principles of hue, value, lightness, and chroma similar to the Munsell color space implementation discussed previously in Section 3.7.

3.8.2 Historical Development of HSV and HSL Color Spaces

In the early 1970s, Richard Shoup and Alvy Ray Smith, at Xerox's Palo Alto Research Center (PARC), pioneered the development of computer

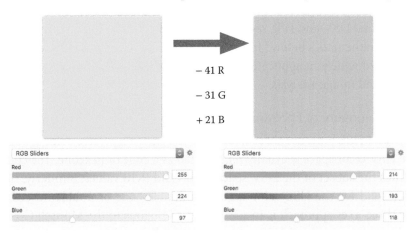

FIGURE 3.15 Illustration of how color specification and modification is not always intuitive when working directly with the RGB values. (Illustration by Theresa-Marie Rhyne, 2015.)

painting programs [36]. Smith conceptualized the HSV color space during this time frame. Smith then moved on to the Computer Graphics Laboratory at the New York Institute of Technology (NYIT) that would later evolve into the Pixar Animation Studios in Emeryville, California. In August 1978, Smith presented his paper on HSV at the annual Association for Computing Machinery's Special Interest Group on Graphics Conference (SIGGRAPH, 1978). The paper, "Color Gamut Transform Pairs," defined HSV and was published in the conference proceedings. George H. Joblove and Donald Greenberg, of Cornell University, also presented the HSL color space and compared it to HSV at SIGGRAPH 1978. The Joblove and Greenberg paper was entitled "Color Spaces for Computer Graphics" [37,38].

The conversions from RGB values to HSV or HSL color spaces could be rapidly computed and easily ran in real time on computer graphics hardware of the late 1970s and early 1980s. By SIGGRAPH 1979, the Computer Graphics Standards Committee recommended and supported these color spaces. Also at SIGGRAPH 1979, Tektronix Inc. introduced computer graphics terminals that relied on HSL for its color designations. The HSV and HSL color spaces, as well as similar ones, were also built into computer graphics software and image editing tools over the years. The ubiquitous nature of these color spaces can be seen in their coverage in fundamental computer graphics textbooks, even today. For example, the editions of the *Computer Graphics: Principles and Practice* review the mathematics behind HSV and HSL [39]. We refer you to this textbook and the original HSV and HSL research papers noted above for further details on the mathematics behind HSV and HSL. Today, HSV and HSL continue to be used widely in applications for color selection in computer graphics design and image analysis.

3.8.3 Geometry of HSV and HSL

HSV and HSL both use three axes to define their respective color spaces. The HSV color space is usually represented as a cone or hexcone. The cone defines the subset of the HSV space with valid RGB values. Similarly, the color solid for the HSL color space is a double cone or double hexcone. The three-axes approach is in some ways analogous to the Munsell Color Order System, covered in Section 3.7. HSV defines hue, saturation, and value, where value is sometimes referred to as brightness. HSL defines hue, saturation, and lightness, where sometimes the order is noted as hue lightness saturation (HLS). We describe these parameters below.

3.8.3.1 Defining Hue

In HSV and HSL, hue is used to describe the degrees of color. The specification of the hue axis ranges from 0 to 360. This forms a color or hue wheel that begins and ends in Red (0/360) and encompasses Yellow (60), Green (120), Cyan (180), Blue (240), and Magenta (300). Examining these specifications more carefully indicates that these hue ranges specifically address the primary colors of the RGB color model for lights and the Cyan Magenta Yellow primary colors of the CMYK color model for printing we noted in Chapter 1. The Red (0/360), Green (120), and Blue (240) RGB hues form a triangle when connected by straight lines on the hue wheel. The same is true for Yellow (60), Cyan (180), and Magenta (300) CMY hues. We will highlight further details about the location of hues on various color wheels in Chapter 4. Figure 3.16 shows specific colors on the hue axis for the HSV and HSL color spaces.

3.8.3.2 Defining Saturation

Saturation indicates the degree that a hue differs from neutral Gray in the color space. It ranges from 0% for no color or desaturation to 100% for a pure color or full saturation. In Figure 3.16, the colors on the outer edge of the hue wheel are pure colors. As we move into the center of the wheel, more Gray is added to the various hues, resulting in the colors dominating less and less. A faded hue or tone indicates the color contains more Gray. At the

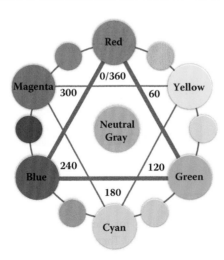

FIGURE 3.16 Diagram of the hue or color wheel that depicts the colors associated with the hue axis in the hue, saturation, and value (HSV) and hue, saturation, and lightness (HSL) color spaces. (Illustration by Theresa-Marie Rhyne, 2015.)

center of the wheel, the neutral Gray zone is reached and no hue dominates. The center of the wheel is the zone of complete desaturation while the outer edge of the hue wheel is the region of full saturation. Saturation has similarities to the chroma parameter of the Munsell Color Order System that we highlighted in Section 3.7. Figure 3.17 shows the degrees of saturation for the Yellow hue ranging from 0% for no color or neutral Gray to 100% for a pure Yellow hue.

3.8.3.3 Defining Value
Value is the brightness of the hue and varies with color saturation in the HSV color model. Value ranges from 0% where the color space is completely Black to 100% where there are colors on the hue wheel. Value is a linear axis running through the center of the hue wheel as shown in Figure 3.18, which also shows the full range for the color Yellow in HSV color space.

3.8.3.4 Defining Lightness
Lightness indicates the level of illumination in the HSL color space. Lightness ranges from 0% for Black (no light) to 100% for full illumination

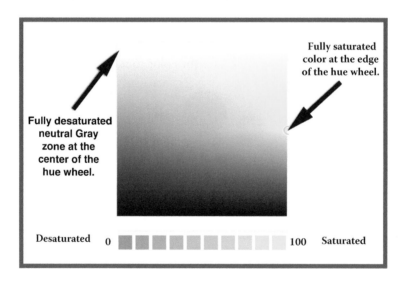

FIGURE 3.17 Degrees of saturation for the Yellow hue in the HSV and HSL color spaces are shown. (Illustration by Theresa-Marie Rhyne, 2015.) Yellow color example generated with the use of the Mozilla Development Network's Color picker tool at https://developer.mozilla.org/en-US/docs/Web/CSS/CSS_Colors /Color_picker_tool.

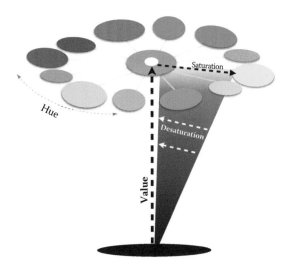

FIGURE 3.18   Geometry of the HSV color space. (Illustration by Theresa-Marie Rhyne, 2015.)

that washes out the hue so it appears as White. Hues at percentages less than 50% appear darker while hues at greater than 50% appear lighter. Figure 3.19 shows that the hue color wheel is located at the 50% value of the lightness scale in the HSL color space. Figure 3.19 also depicts the full range for the color Yellow in the HSL color space.

3.8.4 Comparison of HSV and HSL Color Spaces

HSV and HSL differ in the geometric shape of their color spaces as shown in Figure 3.18 for HSV and Figure 3.19 for HSL. The HSV color space is represented as a single cone while the HSL color space is depicted as a double cone. For both geometric shapes, the central vertical axis represents an achromatic or a neutral axis with Black at the bottom at a value = 0 in HSV and lightness = 0 in HSL. White is at the top of the central axis with value = 1 in HSV and lightness = 0 in HSL. The hue circle of colors is positioned in both color spaces around the edge of the geometric shape at saturation = 1. In HSV, the hue circle is positioned at the top of the cone with a value = 1. In HSL, the hue circle is positioned in the middle of the double cone with lightness = 0.5. This positioning results in some differences in the mixing of the pure colors on the hue circle's outer edge. In HSV, mixing pure colors with White reduces saturation, yielding tints, while mixing pure colors with Black leaves saturation scales unchanged, resulting in shades. With

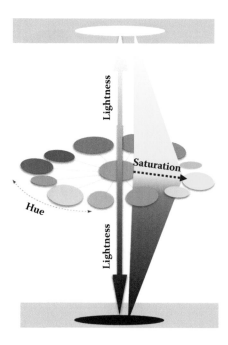

FIGURE 3.19   Geometry of the HSL color space. (Illustration by Theresa-Marie Rhyne, 2015.)

HSL, both tints and shades have full saturation while tones, mixtures of both Black and White, have saturation levels less than 1.

A key advantage to HSV is its conceptual simplicity since each attribute corresponds to color concepts we noted in Chapters 1 and 2. As noted previously, the saturation attribute in HSV corresponds to tinting with desaturated colors having increasing total intensity. This is considered as a limitation to the HSV color space. As a result, the cascading style sheets (CSS) standard for Web content development supports RGB and HSL, but not HSV. We will highlight color standards for the Web in Section 3.9.

HSV and HSL are computationally efficient color spaces for color selection while creating digital content. A key disadvantage of the HSV and HSL color spaces is in regard to addressing the complexity of color appearance such as perceptual uniformity. Both color spaces are not absolute color spaces such as the CIE color spaces covered previously in Section 3.6 or the Munsell color order system covered in Section 3.7. HSV and HSL are defined purely with reference to a given RGB space. As we noted in Section 3.3, there are many commonly applied RGB color spaces. As a result, precise specification of a color involves noting the HSV or HSL attributes as well as the characteristics of the referenced RGB color space and the associated gamut correction in use. Fundamentally, HSV and HSL color spaces tradeoff perceptual uniformity for computational speed. There are many digital content creation situations, such as interactive visualization, real-time virtual environments, or computer game development, where such computational speed is optimal.

3.8.5 Example Color Selection Application Using HSV and HSL

The HSV and HSL color spaces are designed to support effective color *picking* while creating digital media content. Therefore, these color spaces are most commonly applied to color selection tools. Many of these color selection tools provide three sliders for each attribute of the respective color space. Figure 3.20 shows the *Color picker tool*, a free community-built online color selection resource intended for all Web developers and content creators from the Mozilla Development Network (MDN) [40]. In the application, both HSV and HSL color attributes are provided. The Color picker tool is available online at https://developer.mozilla.org/en-US/docs /Web/CSS/CSS_Colors/Color_picker_tool.

In Figure 3.20, we can compare and contrast the HSV and HSL attributes for a Yellow color where the RGB values are R = 237, G = 230, and B = 52. In HSV color space, H = 57, S = 78, and V = 92. In HSL color space, H = 57, S = 83, and L = 56. The hue attribute, H = 57, is constant in both color spaces. The saturation attribute varies slightly between color spaces for this Yellow color. In HSV space, S = 78, while in the HSL space, S = 83. It is anticipated that a color with a value in HSV of 92 would have

RGB: R = 237, G = 230, B = 52

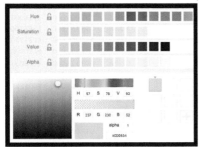 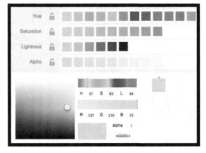

HSV: H = 57, S = 78, V = 92   **HSL: H = 57, S = 83, L = 56**

FIGURE 3.20 Example of a free and online HSV and HSL color selection tool entitled *Color picker tool* (https://developer.mozilla.org/en-US/docs/Web/CSS /CSS_Colors/Color_picker_tool). (Illustration by Theresa-Marie Rhyne, 2015, using the Color picker tool with additional annotations for clarification.)

a Lightness attribute of near-half in the HSL space. With this Yellow color, L = 56 in the HSL space. As to be expected by the geometry of the two color spaces, this Yellow color registers at the top of the HSV color space and in the middle range of the HSL color space. The numerical specifications of these attributes correspond to the geometric differences in HSV and HSL color spaces as diagrammed in Figures 3.18 and 3.19. In the next section, we will highlight the *Color picker tool* further to illustrate color formats associated with Web development.

3.9 WEB COLORS AND HEX TRIPLETS

In developing content for the Web, there are standards for describing and specifying colors for text and graphics. These guidelines are currently monitored and maintained by the World Wide Web Consortium (W3C) [41]. A *Web color* is specified according to its intensity of RGB components. The Web color specifications are based on the sRGB color space that we have discussed in Section 3.3. The sRGB color space was selected since it effectively serves as a best guess for how the majority of monitors, mobile phones, and digital cameras produce color. In setting parameters for displaying Web pages, colors can be defined in the RGB format or in hexadecimal (HEX triplet) format. In some cases, Web colors can also be noted according to their English name. The HEX triplet format, with a leading number sign (#), is the most common format used. Figure 3.21 shows appropriate Web colors on a color wheel with a table noting the English name, RGB value, and HEX triplet value for each hue.

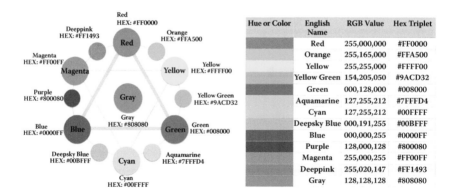

Hue or Color	English Name	RGB Value	Hex Triplet
	Red	255,000,000	#FF0000
	Orange	255,165,000	#FFA500
	Yellow	255,255,000	#FFFF00
	Yellow Green	154,205,050	#9ACD32
	Green	000,128,000	#008000
	Aquamarine	127,255,212	#7FFFD4
	Cyan	127,255,212	#00FFFF
	Deepsky Blue	000,191,255	#00BFFF
	Blue	000,000,255	#0000FF
	Purple	128,000,128	#800080
	Magenta	255,000,255	#FF00FF
	Deeppink	255,020,147	#FF1493
	Gray	128,128,128	#808080

FIGURE 3.21 Web colors on a color wheel. In this illustration, we show appropriate Web colors on a color wheel and provide a table for noting the English name, RGB value, and HEX triplet value for each hue. (Illustration by Theresa-Marie Rhyne, 2016.)

3.9.1 Defining HEX Triplets

A *HEX triplet* is a six-digit and three-byte hexadecimal number used to represent a color in the hypertext markup language (HTML), cascading style sheets (CSS), scalable vector graphics (SVG), extensible 3D graphics (X3D), and other Web applications. The bytes refer to the RGB components of the color where byte 1 refers to the Red value, byte 2 refers to the Green value, and byte 3 refers to the Blue value. Hexadecimal notation uses 16 distinct symbols where 0–9 represent values zero to nine and A, B, C, D, E, and F represent values 10–15. For a Web color, one byte represents a number in the range of 00 to FF. Using our previous example in Figure 3.19, for the Yellowish color where R = 237, G = 230, and B = 52 in RGB color space, the hexadecimal numbers are ED, E6, and 34. The HEX triplet value is noted as #EDE634, where the hexadecimal numbers are concatenated together. If any of the three bytes has a color value that is less than 16 (in hexadecimal notation) or 10 (in decimal notation), it must be represented with a leading zero so that the triplet always has six digits. For example, pure Yellow, where R = 255, G = 255, and B = 0 has a HEX triplet value of #FFFF00. It takes 24 bytes to specify a given color in this notation system and the total number of colors that can be specified is 256 to the exponential power of 3 or 16,777,216. Today, the majority of color selection tools automatically convert between RGB and HEX triplet values. This is true of the Color picker tool. Figure 3.22 shows the full user

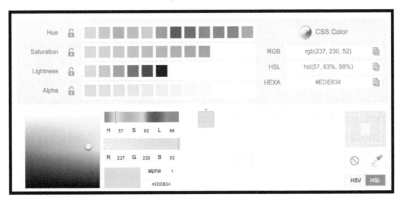

RGB: R = 237, G = 230, B = 52   HSL: H = 57, S = 83, L = 56   HEX: #EDE634

FIGURE 3.22 Example color selection tool with Web colors specified in the RGB, HSL, and HEX triplet values using the Color picker tool (https://developer .mozilla.org/en-US/docs/Web/CSS/CSS_Colors/Color_picker_tool). (Illustration by Theresa-Marie Rhyne, 2015, using the Color picker tool with additional annotations for clarification.)

interface of the Color picker tool where the RGB, HSL, and HEX triplet values are noted together for the Yellowish color of R = 237, G = 230, and B = 52 or #EDE634 [42].

3.9.2 HTML, CSS, and SVG Web Colors

HTML, CSS, and SVG are key technologies for creating Web pages. HTML provides the foundation or the structure for the Web page. CSS defines the page's presentation, including colors, fonts, and layout. SVG is the W3C open standard for supporting two-dimensional graphics in Web pages including interactivity and animation. The *CSS Color Module* recommendation is the guiding document in regard to applying color to Web pages and is available online at http://www.w3.org/TR/css3-color/. At the time of the writing of this book, the CSS Color Module Level 3 recommendation, as of June 2, 2011, is in effect. The HTML and SVG standards reference back to the CSS Color Module Level 3 recommendation [43,44]. In addition to describing the color keywords as well as the RGB and HEX triplet formats for specifying Web colors, the CSS Color Module also outlines how to specify Web colors according to the HSL color model. We covered HSL in the Section 3.7. As shown in Figure 3.22, the Color picker tool we highlighted previously includes a *CSS Color* section that specifies colors in RGB, HSL, and HEX triplet formats to match the W3C color guidelines. Most color selection tools and apps include RGB and HEX triplet formats at a minimum.

3.9.3 Web Safe Colors

Web safe colors consist of 216 colors that have solid, nondithered, and consistent display on any display device supporting at least 8-bit color (256 colors). Today's display technologies typically support 24-bit color or better so the need for Web safe color consideration is becoming obsolete. However, we review the Web safe concepts here.

Historically, many computer monitors were capable of displaying in only 8-bit color that included only 256 colors. If an image or graphic contained a color not within the 256 colors of the display monitor, a substitute color was applied or dithering was used to try to approximate the color. Using the substitute color option often resulted in the closest color being applied with unexpected results frequently occurring. The dithering solution slowed down the loading of the graphic or image due to the calculations involved in creating the color. To avoid this situation, a set of *Web safe colors* became necessary. The number of 216 web safe colors was selected since computer operating systems typically reserved 16–20 colors for their own use. The number

216 also allowed for six equally spaced shades for RGB values from 0 to 255 and also supported the 00 to FF range in a hexadecimal notation (HEX triplets). This mathematical relationship can be simply noted as $6 \times 6 \times 6 = 216$.

The Web safe colors developed were based on mathematics and not aesthetics or color theory. The 216 colors contain RGB values of 0, 51, 102, 153, 204, and 255, where RGB values range from 0 to 255. These numbers are multiples of 51 or 20% of 255 and result in the six equally spaced shades of RGB values at 0%, 20%, 40%, 60%, 80%, and 100% as we noted above. In the HEX triplet equivalents, the 216 colors contain HEX values of 00, 33, 66, 99, CC, and FF. Many look-up tables have been developed that present the entire range of the 216 web safe colors. Two excellent resources are at http://websafe-colors.info/ and http://cloford.com/resources/colours/websafe1.htm [45,46].

As stated earlier in this section, web safe colors have become an obsolete concept since modern display devices now support 24-bit color levels or better. As we have shown, the concept is based on mathematics and not aesthetics or color theory. However, it is helpful to be aware of the Web safe terminology and the rationale behind its usage.

3.9.4 An Example of Color Capture and Web Color Selection with a Mobile App

There are many mobile and online apps that allow for selecting colors from an existing graphics file or digital photograph. The colors selected usually appear as color swatches with the Web color noted in the RGB and HEX triplet formats. Here, we show how to select colors with the Color Companion mobile app, from Digital Media Interactive LLC, for the iPhone or iPad. This app is available for purchase from the iTunes store and more details are noted at https://itunes.apple.com/us/app/color-companion-analyzer-converter/id477794973?mt=8 [47].

For this example, we import a digital photograph from our iPhone directly into the Color Companion app. The image is of a spring garden. Color Companion analyzes the image and determines colors for us to select as a possible color palette. We select a palette of four colors from the digital image. This selection process is shown in the middle image of Figure 3.23. After naming and saving the color palette, we can scroll down to see the four Web colors of our color scheme as HEX triplets. For our example, we saved the color palette as *Spring Garden*.

The right-hand side image of Figure 3.23 shows the HEX triplets of the Spring Garden color scheme. Color Companion also provides the RGB, Lab, HSB, and CMYK values of the four colors selected. We discussed the

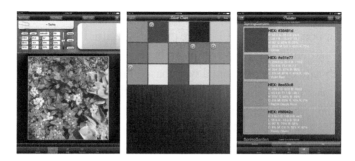

FIGURE 3.23   Using a mobile app to select Web colors. (Illustration by Theresa-Marie Rhyne, 2016, using a personal digital photograph with the Color Companion App from Digital Media Interactive LLC.)

various color systems associated with these values in previous sections of this chapter. Please see Section 3.6.2 for a discussion on CIE LAB, referred to here as Lab, values. In Section 3.8, we provide a discussion on the HSV color model that is frequently referred to as the HSB model, as shown in this Color Companion example. In Chapter 4, we discuss further how to build color schemes and the principles of color harmony.

3.10 PANTONE COLOR MATCHING SYSTEM

The *Pantone color matching system* (PMS) is a proprietary color space used primarily in printing and also in a wide range of other industries, including cosmetics, colored paint, fabric, and plastics. Pantone matching methods have evolved into a standardized color reproduction system that utilizes the Pantone numbering system to identify colors [48]. Individuals located in different geographic locations can refer to particular PMS values to ensure that colors match without making a direct personal contact with each other. The Pantone color guides consist of narrow cardboard sheets (approximately 6 by 2 in or 15 by 5 cm) that are printed on one side with rectangular samples showing the different Pantone colors. The guide is bound together at one end to allow for opening the strips out in a fan like manner. Additionally, Pantone provides binders with rectangular swatches and digital media resources [49]. In 2009, Pantone released the myPantone app for iOS platforms and later extended it to Android devices. In August 2016, the PANTONE Studio app for iOS platforms became available. We will highlight the mobile PANTONE Studio app for iOS platforms later on in Section 3.10.3. See Figure 3.24 for an illustration of a virtual Pantone fan deck used in the previous myPantone app and how it has transitioned to digital color swatches in the PANONE Studio app.

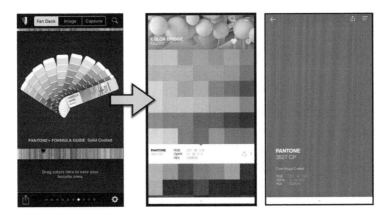

FIGURE 3.24 Progression from the virtual fan deck of the older myPantone app to the new digital swatches of the PANTONE Studio app. (Illustration by Theresa-Marie Rhyne, 2016, using the older myPantone and new PANTONE Studio apps from Pantone.)

3.10.1 Evolution of the Pantone Matching System

The origins of Pantone go back to the 1950s when Lawrence Herbert joined a small commercial printing company, M&J Levine Advertising [50–52]. Herbert used his chemistry background to simplify the company's production of inks to a set of 12 stock pigments from a full range of colors. By 1962, Herbert was leading the printing division that was profitable while other aspects of M&J Levine Advertising were not. Herbert purchased the printing division and renamed it to Pantone in 1962. The first Pantone Matching System Printer's Edition was introduced in 1963. By the end of the 1970s, PMS had become a standard in wide international usage. In 1984, Pantone formed its Electronic Color Systems Division to reproduce its color management system into a digital format. In the 1990s, Pantone partnered with leading hardware and software companies to pioneer color management of digital media and printing. By the 2000s, Pantone was a recognized leader in color management and began providing translations of their PMS values to sRGB and Lab formats. In 2007, X-Rite Inc, a supplier of color measurement equipment, purchased Pantone Inc. In 2009, the myPantone app for the iPhone became available for purchase from the iTunes store. Later, a myPantone version for the Android platform became available. On August 2, 2016, the current PANTONE Studio app became available for the iOS platform. [53,54]. The Pantone LLC continues today as a subsidiary of X-Rite, with its Web site at http://www.pantone.com. Interestingly, both Pantone LLC and the Munsell Color Company, highlighted previously in this chapter, are currently subsidiaries of X-Rite Inc.

3.10.2 Supporting CMYK Color Printing

A frequent use of PMS values is in standardizing colors in the CMYK printing process. We highlighted the CMYK color model in Section 1.2. There is a specified subset of Pantone colors that are reproducible in the CMYK printing process. Designers select colors from this subset and note their PMS values for various stages of the CMYK color printing and reproduction process. It is important to note that a majority of the Pantone Matching System's colors cannot be reproduced with the CMYK process but are created with the use of designated base pigments mixed in specified amounts. Understanding the subset of Pantone colors that the CMYK process can reproduce becomes important if it is desired to stay within range of the CMYK printing process and not yield unexpected results.

3.10.3 Applying Color Theory Concepts with the PANTONE Studio App

As mentioned earlier in this section, the PANTONE Studio app is a mobile or pocket application available for iOS platforms. As of the writing of this book, the Android version remains under development and is anticipated to be available from the GooglePlay online store. The iOS version is available from the iTunes store. The PANTONE Studio app is "free" at a basic level. A $7.99 monthly subscription provides access to a complete library of Pantone colors, values and references. More information about the PANTONE Studio app is available from the Pantone Web site: (https://www.pantone.com/studio).

The app provides digital display of color swatches for creating a color palette from scratch. Moving your finger along the color display allows for locating specific Pantone hues. Tapping on a swatch displays the color in a detailed view. A selected Pantone color can be dragged into the palette zone to store it. Once the Pantone color is in the palette zone, tapping on it reveals the sRGB and HTML (HEX triplet) values as well as the CMYK data. In Figure 3.24, we selected a Magenta hue called Pantone 3527 CP. The sRGB values are 201, 46, and 133. The HTML (HEX value) is #C92E85. The CMYK values are 11, 90, 0, and 0. Since we have selected a Magenta hue, it is not surprising that the M (Magenta) number in the CMYK values equals 90. We have covered the sRGB color space in Section 3.3, and the

HEX triplet values in Section 3.9.1. The CMYK color model was presented in Chapter 1. Figure 3.24 shows the PANTONE Studio app implementation of these color theory concepts for everyday usage.

3.10.4 Color Capture from a Digital Image with PANTONE Studio

The PANTONE Studio app also allows for capturing colors from a digital image or photograph on your mobile phone. We show an example in Figure 3.25. PANTONE Studio provides four main options: "Colors", "Images", "Articles" and "Studio". The Colors option allow for selecting individual colors as we did in Section 3.10.3. The Images option allows for working with stored photos. The Articles option features information from the Pantone Color Institute. The Studio option shows how your color palette will appear in various design templates. Once the Images option is selected, the PANTONE Studio app automatically suggests five Pantone colors matched to dominant colors in the stored images of your camera roll. It is also possible to move around the image sensor or big dots to select a specific hue with the PANTONE Studio app, changing the five Pantone hue options of the designated color palette at the top. The PANTONE Studio app also provides a Harmonies option for a selected Pantone color. We will cover harmony in Chapter 4 and explore the PANTONE studio app further in Chapter 5. Figure 3.25 presents the Pantone color capture process for the *Spring Garden* image we examined earlier in Figure 3.23.

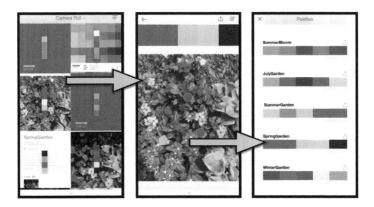

FIGURE 3.25 Color capture from an image with the PANTONE Studio app. (Illustration by Theresa-Marie Rhyne, 2015, using a personal digital photograph with the PANTONE Studio app from Pantone.)

3.11 CONCLUDING REMARKS

In this chapter, we reviewed the concepts of color gamut, color spaces, and color systems. The color spaces reviewed in this chapter are used widely in color reproduction and color standards. This chapter has provided the terminology to understand online and mobile color apps that allow for digital color selection and capture. It is important to continue to remember a key concept about color gamut: Viewing a color in digital or virtual color spaces does not always mean that the color will appear the same in printed or physical color spaces. This is because of the differences in the RGB color model for display, the CMYK color model for printing, and the RYB color model for painting that we highlighted in Chapters 1 and 2. In Chapter 4, we will examine concepts of color harmony that pertain to all three of these color models.

REFERENCES

1. Ibraheem, N.A., Hasan, M.M., Khan, R.Z., and Mishra, P.K. (2012). Understanding color models: A review. *ARPN Journal of Science and Technology*, 2(3): 265–275.
2. Schanda, J. (ed.) (2007). *Colorimetry: Understanding the CIE System*. Hoboken, NJ: John Wiley & Sons.
3. Susstrunk, S., Buckley, R., and Swen, S. (1999). Standard RGB Color Spaces. Proceedings of the IS&T/SID Seventh Color Imaging Conference (ISBN: 0-89208-224-0). Springfield, VA: IS&T/SID, pp. 127–134.
4. Schewe, J. and Fraser, B. (2004). A Color Managed Raw Workflow—From Camera to Final Print. Whitepaper. Available at https://www.adobe.com /digitalimag/pdfs/color_managed_raw_workflow.pdf, accessed June 11, 2016.
5. Hoffman, N. (2011). 2011 Color and Imaging Conference, Part VI: Special Session on Revisiting Color Spaces. Real Time Rendering Blog. Available at http://www.realtimerendering.com/blog/2011-color-and-imaging -conference-part-vi-specialsession/, accessed March 10, 2016.
6. Stone, M. (2003). Color Vision. *A Field Guide to Digital Color*. Canada: A.K. Peters/CRC Press, pp. 1–19.
7. Fairman, H.S., Brill, M.H., and Hemmendinger, H. (1997). How the CIE 1931 color-matching functions were derived from Wright-Guild data. *Color Research and Application*, 22(1): 11–27.
8. Wright, W.D. (2007). Professor Wright's paper from the golden jubilee book: The historical and experimental background to the 1931 CIE system of colorimetry. In J. Schanda (ed.), *Colorimetry: Understanding the CIE System*. Hoboken, NJ: John Wiley & Sons, pp. 9–23.
9. MacAdam, D.L. (1942). Visual sensitivities to color differences in daylight. *Journal of the Optical Society of America*, 32(5): 247–274.
10. Sharma, G. (2002). Color fundamentals for digital imaging. In G. Sharma and R. Bala (eds.), *Digital Color Imaging Handbook*. Boca Raton, FL: CRC Press, pp. 2–97.

11. Sharma, G. and Bala, R. (eds.) (2002). *Digital Color Imaging Handbook*. Boca Raton, FL: CRC Press.
12. Ohta, N. (1977). Correspondence between CIELAB and CIELUV color differences. *Color Research and Application*, 2(4): 178–182.
13. Olean, C. (2001). Comparisons between color-space scales, uniform-color-scale atlases, and color-difference formulae. *Color Research and Application*, 26(5): 351–361.
14. Adams, E.Q. (1942). X-Z planes in the 1931 I.C.I. system of colorimetry. *Journal of Optical Society of America*, 32(3): 168–173.
15. Nickerson, D. and Stultz, K.F. (1944). Color tolerance specification. *Journal of the Optical Society of America*, 34(9): 550–570.
16. Hunt, R.W.G. and Pointer, M.R. (2011). *Measuring Color*, Fourth Edition. Chichester, United Kingdom: John Wiley & Sons Ltd.
17. Hunter Labs. (1996). Hunter Lab Color Scale, Applications Note, Hunter Association Laboratory, Inc. Resto, Virginia, 8(9): 1–4.
18. Hunter Labs. (2012). Measuring Color using Hunter L, a, b versus CIE 1976 L*a*b*. Available at www.hunterlab.com/de/an-1005-de.pdf, accessed March 23, 2016.
19. Munsell Color. (2015). Munsell Books of Color, X-Rite Inc. Available at http://munsell.com/color-products/colorcommunications-products/munsell -books-and-sheets/, accessed April 25, 2016.
20. Munsell, A.H. (1905). *A Color Notation*. Boston, MA: G.H. Ellis Company.
21. Munsell, A.H. (1915). *Atlas of the Munsell Color System*. Malden, MA: Wadsworth, Howland & Co., Inc.
22. Cleland, T.M., Munsell, A.H., and Strathmore Paper Company. (1921). *A Grammar of Color: Arrangements of Strathmore Papers in a Variety of Printed Color Combinations According to the Munsell Color System*. Mittineague, MA: Strathmore Paper Co.
23. Nickerson, D. (1976). History of the Munsell color system, company, and foundation. I. *Color Research and Application*, 1(3): 7–10.
24. Nickerson, D. (1976). History of the Munsell color system, company and foundation. II. Its scientific application. *Color Research and Application*, 1(2): 69–77.
25. Nickerson, D. (1976). History of the Munsell color system, company and foundation. III. *Color Research and Application*, 1(3): 121–130.
26. Kuehni, R.G. (2002). The early development of the Munsell system. *Color Research and Application*, 27(1): 20–27.
27. Landa, E.R. and Fairchild, M.D. (2005). Charting color from the eye of the beholder. *American Scientist*, 93(5): 436–443. doi:10.1511/2005.5.436.
28. MacEvoy, B. (2005). Modern Color Models—Munsell Color System, Color Vision, part of the Handprint.com Web site. Available at http://www .handprint.com/HP/WCL/color7.html#MUNSELL, accessed April 13, 2016.
29. American Society of Testing Materials. (1968). ASTM D1535: Specifying Color by the Munsell System. Available at https://archive.org/details/gov .law.astm.d1535.1968, accessed April 23, 2016.

30. Munsell Color Company. (2015). Defining Color Systems for Precise Color Validation, X-Rite Inc. Available at https://www.xrite.com/documents /literature/en/L10-315_Defining_Color_Munsell_en.pdf, accessed June 11, 2016.

31. Indow, T. and Aoki, N. (1983). Multidimensional mapping of 178 Munsell colors. *Color Research and Application*, 8(3): 145–152.

32. Briggs, D. (2007). The Dimensions of Colour—The Dimension of Chroma, Color Vision, part of the HueValueChomra Web site. Available at http:// www.huevaluechroma.com/082.php, accessed June 11, 2016.

33. Munsell Color Science Laboratory. (2015). Munsell Renotation Data, Chester F. Carlson Center for Imaging Science at the Rochester Institute of Technology. Available at http://www.cis.rit.edu/research/mcsl2/online /munsell.php, accessed June 11, 2016.

34. WallkillColor. (2015). Munsell Conversion Software. Available at http:// www.wallkillcolor.com, accessed June 11, 2016.

35. Silicon Goblin Technologies. (2012). Munsell DG—iTunes Preview. Available at https://itunes.apple.com/us/app/munselldg/id515717868?mt=8, accessed June 11, 2016.

36. Shoup, R. (2001). SuperPaint: An early frame buffer graphics system. *IEEE Annals of the History of Computing*, 23(2): 32–37.

37. Smith, A.R. (1978). Color Gamut Transform Pairs. SIGGRAPH '78 Proceedings of the Fifth Annual Conference on Computer Graphics and Interactive Techniques. New York, NY, ACM, pp. 12–19.

38. Joblove, G.H. and Greenberg, D. (1978). Color Spaces for Computer Graphics. SIGGRAPH '78 Proceedings of the Fifth Annual Conference on Computer Graphics and Interactive Techniques. New York, NY, ACM, pp. 20–25.

39. Hughes, J.F., Van Dam, A., McGuire, M., Sklar, D.F., Foley, J.D., Feiner, S.K, and Akeley, K. (2013). *Computer Graphics: Principles and Practice*, Third Edition. Boston, MA: Addison-Wesley Professional.

40. Shepherd, E.T., Ivanica, G., and The Mozilla Development Network. (2015). Color Picker Tool. Available at https://developer.mozilla.org/en-US/docs /Web/CSS/CSS_Colors/Color_picker_tool., accessed June 11, 2016.

41. World Wide Web Consortium. (2015). HTML & CSS, part of the W3C's standards web site. Available at http://www.w3.org/standards /webdesign/htmlcss, accessed June 11, 2016.

42. Lilley, C., Grasso, A., and The World Wide Web Consortium. (2008). SVG Color 1.2, Part 2: Language, part of the W3C's standards Web site. Available at http://www.w3.org/TR/2009/WD-SVGColor12-20091001/, accessed June 11, 2016.

43. Celik, T., Lilley, C., and David Baron, L. (2011). CSS Color Module Level 3, part of the W3C's standards web site. Available at http://www.w3.org/TR /css3-color/, accessed June 11, 2016.

44. Bellamy-Royds, A. and Cagle, K. (2015). *SVG Colors, Patterns & Gradients: Painting Vector Graphics*. Sebastopol, CA: O'Reilly Media.

45. Cloford.com. (2015). Web-Safe Colours. Available at http://cloford.com /resources/colours/websafe1.htm, accessed June 11, 2016.

46. WEBSAFECOLORS. (2015). 216 Web Safe Colors. Available at http://websafecolors.info/, accessed June 11, 2016.
47. Digital Media Interactive LLC. (2016). Color Companion—Analyzer & Converter. Available at https://itunes.apple.com/us/app/color-companion-analyzer-converter/id477794973?mt=8, accessed June 11, 2016.
48. Pantone. (2016). The Pantone Matching System. Available at https://www.pantone.com/the-pantone-matching-system, accessed June 11, 2016.
49. Pantone. (2016). Pantone Colours. Available at http://www.pantone-colours.com/, accessed June 11, 2016.
50. Designface for Pantone. (2016). The History of Pantone. Available at http://www.designface.co.uk/content/pantonehistory, accessed June 11, 2016.
51. FundingUniverse. (2016). Pantone Inc. History. Available at http://www.fundinguniverse.com/companyhistories/pantone-inc-history/, accessed March 11, 2016.
52. Kennedy, P. (2013). Who made that Pantone chip. *New York Times Magazine*. Available at http://www.nytimes.com/2013/02/24/magazine/who-made-that-pantone-chip.html?_r=3, accessed June 11, 2016.
53. Pantone. (2016). Introducing Pantone Studio. Available at https://www.pantone.com/studio, accessed August 3, 2016.
54. Co.Design. (2016). Pantone's Addictive New App Turns The World Into A Prismatic Palette. Available at http://www.fastcodesign.com/3062394/pantones-addictive-new-app-turns-the-world-into-a-prismatic-palette, accessed August 3, 2016.

CHAPTER 4

Defining Color Harmony

4.1 COLOR WHEELS

Color wheels are tools that depict color relationships by organizing colors in a circle to visualize how the hues relate to each other. Many color wheels are based on three primary colors, three secondary colors, and the six intermediate or tertiary colors formed by mixing a primary with a secondary color. This results in 12 hues on the color wheel. Some color wheels have even finer divisions, resulting in 24 colors being depicted. The primary colors are the core of a color model and cannot be mixed. The secondary colors are mixtures of the primary colors. Figure 3.16 depicts colors associated with the hue, saturation, and value (HSV) and hue, saturation, and lightness (HSL) color spaces, and is a typical example of the 12 hues configuration. Other color wheels examples include four opponent colors and can have four or eight main colors. Figure 2.4 that diagramed Ewald Hering's opponent color theory is an example of a color wheel with four main colors. The Munsell color order system includes five primary hues and five secondary hues. We diagrammed the Munsell hue circle with a total of 40 hue divisions in Figure 3.11. In this chapter, we will look further into the steps of constructing a color wheel, examine color harmony between hues on the wheel, and highlight some historical and current evolutions of the color wheel such as color gamut masking. There are many other books and online references on color harmony. References [1–4] provide additional reading on the principals of color harmony.

4.2 STEPS IN CONSTRUCTING A COLOR WHEEL

There are four steps in constructing a color wheel: (1) define the color model and place the resulting primaries equidistantly on the wheel, (2) determine the resulting secondary colors that are mixtures of the primary colors and place the secondary colors equidistantly between the primaries on the wheel, (3) establish the tertiary colors that are mixtures of primary and secondary hues and place the tertiary colors equidistantly between the primary and secondary colors, and (4) refine the color wheel with additional equidistant divisions and neutral colors if desired. We will work through these four steps for the three color models we defined in Chapter 1: (1) the Red, Green, and Blue (RGB) display color model; (2) the Cyan, Magenta, Yellow, and Key Black (CMYK) printers color model; and (3) the Red, Yellow, and Blue (RYB) painters color model.

4.2.1 Geometry of the RGB Display Color Wheel

Step 1 is easily determined for the RGB display model with the primary colors being Red, Green, and Blue. We place these three colors clockwise and equidistantly from each other. We learned step 2 in Chapter 1 with the secondary colors being the combination of Red and Green to equal Yellow, Green and Blue to equal Cyan, and Blue and Red to equal Magenta. We place these secondary colors clockwise and equidistantly between the primary RGB colors. For step 3, the tertiary colors are Red Yellow (Orange), Yellow Green (Lime), Green Cyan (Aqua Marine), Cyan Blue (Deep Sky Blue), Blue Magenta (Purple), and Magenta Red (Deep Pink). We place these tertiary colors in clockwise respective locations on the wheel between the primary and secondary colors. For step 4, neutral Gray is the combination of two colors opposing one another on the wheel such as Red and Cyan. So, we place Gray in the center. We show these steps in Figure 4.1.

4.2.2 Geometry of the CMYK Printers Color Wheel

The geometry of the CMYK printers color wheel is the inverse of the RGB display color wheel. For step 1, the primary colors are Cyan, Magenta, and Yellow. We place these three colors clockwise and equidistant from each other. In step 2, the three secondary colors are the combination of Cyan and Magenta to equal Blue, the combination of Magenta and Yellow to yield Red, and the combination of Yellow and Cyan to equal Green. We place these secondary colors clockwise and equidistantly between the primary CMY colors. For step 3, the tertiary colors are Cyan Blue (Deep

FIGURE 4.1   Steps for building the Red, Green, and Blue (RGB) color wheel. (Image created by Theresa-Marie Rhyne, 2016.)

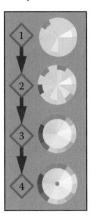

FIGURE 4.2   Steps for building the Cyan, Magenta, Yellow, and Key Black (CMYK) color wheel. (Image created by Theresa-Marie Rhyne, 2016.)

Sky Blue), Blue Magenta (Purple), Magenta Red (Deep Pink), Red Yellow (Orange), Yellow Green (Lime), and Green Cyan (Aqua Marine). We place these tertiary colors in clockwise respective locations on the wheel between the primary and secondary colors. For step 4, Gray is the combination of two colors opposing one another on the wheel such as Cyan and Red. So, we place Gray at the center of the circle. These steps are shown in Figure 4.2.

4.2.3 Geometry of the RYB Painters Color Wheel

The RYB color wheel provides a guide to developing color palettes for art compositions. It is based on how artists have naturally combined paint color pigments for centuries with minerals from the earth. The RYB color

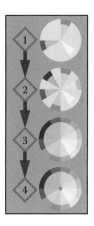

FIGURE 4.3 Steps for building the Red, Yellow, and Blue (RYB) color wheel. (Image created by Theresa-Marie Rhyne, 2016.)

wheel is frequently the first color wheel we learned in our own childhood education while mixing our paint colors. The RYB color palette has more earth tones to it than the RGB color palette created from lights and the CMYK color palette created from printing inks. For step 1 in building the RYB color wheel, the primary colors are Red, Yellow, and Blue. In step 2, the secondary colors are the combination of Red and Yellow to produce Orange, the combination of Yellow and Blue to produce Green, and the combination of Blue and Red to produce Purple. We place these secondary colors clockwise and equidistantly between the primary RYB colors. For step 3, the tertiary colors are Red Orange, Orange Yellow, Yellow Green, Green Blue, Blue Purple and Purple Red. We place these tertiary colors in clockwise respective locations on the wheel between the primary and secondary colors. For step 4, as in our previous examples, Gray is the combination of two colors opposing one another on the wheel such as Red and Green. So, we place Gray in the center of the wheel. These steps are shown in Figure 4.3.

4.2.4 Comparing the RGB, CMYK, and RYB Color Wheels

The RGB additive and the CMYK subtractive color wheels are composed of the same hues and are the inverse combinations of each other, as we noted in Figure 1.6. So, one color wheel will suffice as we focus on defining color harmony concepts Sections 4.3 through 4.5. For further discussion in this chapter, we will reference the RGB/CMYK color wheel. The RGB/CMYK and RYB color wheels differ in the hues for each respective color

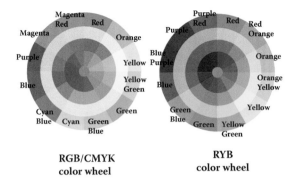

FIGURE 4.4   Comparison of the RGB/CMYK and RYB color wheels. (Image created by Theresa-Marie Rhyne, 2016.)

shown. Historically, many aspects of color theory were developed by artists and designers based on the RYB color wheel. We will highlight some of this evolution later in this chapter. As we noted in Chapter 1, the RYB subtractive color model is similar but different from either of the RGB and CMYK models. In applying color theory to digital media, it becomes helpful to understand both the RGB/CMYK and RYB color wheels for effective application and communication of color harmony. Figure 4.4 compares the RGB/CMYK and RYB color wheels side by side.

4.3 DEFINING HUES, TINTS, TONES, AND SHADES ON THE COLOR WHEEL

As we noted when reviewing color spaces in Chapter 3, a color is defined in terms of it specific parameters such as hue, value, and chroma in the Munsell color order systems or hue saturation and value in the HSV color space. For a detailed color wheel, there are four rings of concentric circles that represent the elements of *hues*, *tints*, *tones*, and *shades*. We define each of these elements below and visually summarize them in Figure 4.4.

4.3.1 Hues

As in the color spaces that we discussed in Chapter 3, a *hue* is the brightest or purest form of a color and resides on the outermost part of the color wheel. In Figure 4.5, the outer rim of colors represented in the RGB/CMYK and the RYB wheels are the hues.

4.3.2 Tints

A *tint* is defined as a hue mixed with White. Tints can vary from small to large percentages of White mixed with the original hue. Figure 4.6 shows

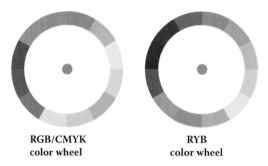

RGB/CMYK
color wheel

RYB
color wheel

FIGURE 4.5   The hues on the RGB/CMYK and RYB color wheels. Hues are shown on the outer rim of the wheel and are the brightest and purest colors. (Image created by Theresa-Marie Rhyne, 2016.)

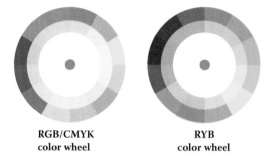

RGB/CMYK
color wheel

RYB
color wheel

FIGURE 4.6   The tints on the RGB/CMYK and RYB color wheels. Tints are represented as the second circle next to the hues on the wheel. Tints are defined as a hue mixed with White. (Image created by Theresa-Marie Rhyne, 2016.)

the tints as the second circle next to the hues of the RGB/CMYK and the RYB wheels. We used 50% hue and 50% White to form the tints shown in the wheels.

4.3.3 Tones

A *tone* is a hue mixed with true Gray. A hue mixed with any amount of Gray is called a tone of the hue. Figure 4.7 shows the tones as the third concentric ring on of the RGB/CMYK and the RYB wheels. We used 50% hue and 50% Gray to form the tints shown in the wheels.

4.3.4 Shades

A *shade* is defined as a hue mixed with Black. Just as with tints and tones, a shade can vary from small to large percentages of Black mixed with the original hue. In Figure 4.8, the fourth and inner most concentric ring of

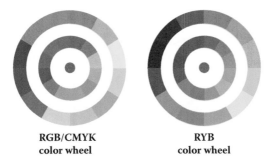

RGB/CMYK
color wheel

RYB
color wheel

FIGURE 4.7   The tones on the RGB/CMYK and RYB color wheels. Tones of hues are represented as the third circle or ring on the wheel. Tones are defined as a hue mixed with Gray. (Image created by Theresa-Marie Rhyne, 2016.)

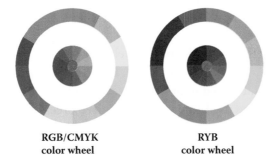

RGB/CMYK
color wheel

RYB
color wheel

FIGURE 4.8   The shades on the RGB/CMYK and RYB color wheels. Shades of hues are represented as the inner most circle or ring on the wheel. Shades are defined as a hue mixed with Black. (Image created by Theresa-Marie Rhyne, 2016.)

the RGB/CMYK and the RYB wheels depicts shades of the various hues. We used 50% hue and 50% Black to form the tints shown in the wheels.

4.4 WARM AND COOL COLORS ON COLOR WHEELS

The color wheel can be divided into *warm and cool* colors. In general, Green, Blue, and Purple are defined as cool colors, while Yellow, Orange, and Red are grouped as warm colors. Warm colors tend to advance and expand in space. Cool colors tend to recede and contract in space. White, Gray, and Black are considered to be neutral in this regard. As a result, colors can have physiological and psychological effects on people. Wassily Kandinsky, in 1910, published detailed writings on these effects of color in his *Concerning the Spiritual in Art* essay [5]. Two colors can also have a relative color temperature with regard to one another. For

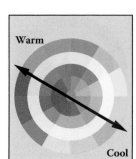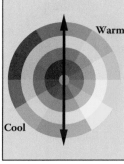

RGB/CMYK color wheel   RYB color wheel

FIGURE 4.9   The division of warm and cool colors on the RGB/CMYK and RYB color wheels. (Image created by Theresa-Marie Rhyne, 2016.)

example, on the RGB/CMYK color wheel, Magenta is considered a hotter color against its adjacent cooler Purple. In RYB color space, a warm Red Orange color can be used to project a crackling fire while its Green Blue complement can be used to project a calm sea breeze. Figure 4.9 shows the division of warm and cool colors on the RGB/CMYK and RYB color wheels, respectively.

4.5 COLOR HARMONY

Color harmony is the process of choosing colors that work well together in the composition of an image. Similar to concepts in music, there are *color cords* on the color wheel that help to provide common guidelines for how hues will work together. These color cords are generalized recommendations with the final color selection dependent on specific parameters associated with the design project. An important aspect in working with color harmony is determining a key color to build the harmonies around. We define basic cords on the color wheel that represent color harmony in the key hue of Yellow below.

For each harmony, we work through an example that applies these concepts. In our examples, we frequently work with the hues, tints, tones, and shades principles to create variations in color selection. The examples shown here are basic infographics or information visualization charts that can be generated with software tools such as Microsoft Excel or Word, Apple Numbers or Pages, Google Docs, Tableau Software, and many others. For our examples, we used the chart functions in Apple Numbers and Apple Pages. We use a sample data set of sales over a 4-month period.

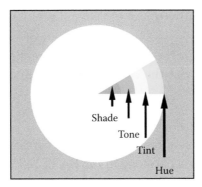

FIGURE 4.10   Monochromatic color harmony in the key of Yellow. (Image created by Theresa-Marie Rhyne, 2016.)

We apply color harmonies in the key of Yellow within RGB/CMYK color space.

4.5.1 Monochromatic Harmony

Monochromatic harmony uses one hue and various tints, tones, and shades associated with that one hue. In Figure 4.10, we establish Yellow as our key color and include a tint, tone, and shade of the selected hue.

4.5.1.1 Example of Monochromatic Harmony

In this example, we develop a pie chart of sales data over 4 months and apply a monochromatic harmony in the key of Yellow. With monochromatic harmony, we use a single hue and its tints, tones, and shades to produce the color variance. Figure 4.11 shows our pie chart with Yellow monochromatic harmony.

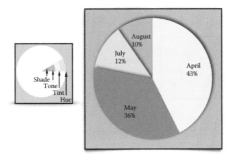

FIGURE 4.11   Example of monochromatic harmony. (Image created by Theresa-Marie Rhyne, 2016.)

4.5.2 Analogous Harmony

Analogous harmony is based on the concept of three colors that are next to each other on the color wheel. Figure 4.12 shows analogous harmony with Yellow at the center for the RGB/CMYK and the RYB color wheels.

4.5.2.1 Example of Analogous Harmony

Here, we develop a three-dimensional bar chart of sales data over 4 months and apply an analogous harmony in the key of Yellow. For this example, we select the Yellow hue, the Orange hue on its left, and the Yellow Green hue on its right. We use shades of each of the three colors. Figure 4.13 shows our three-dimensional bar chart with a Yellow analogous harmony that includes shades of Orange, Yellow, and Yellow Green hues.

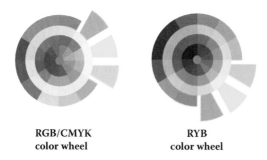

RGB/CMYK
color wheel

RYB
color wheel

FIGURE 4.12 Analogous color harmony in the key of Yellow. (Image created by Theresa-Marie Rhyne, 2016.)

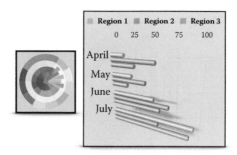

FIGURE 4.13 Example of analogous harmony. (Image created by Theresa-Marie Rhyne, 2016.)

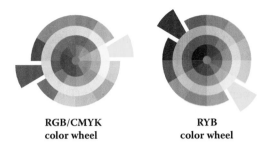

RGB/CMYK
color wheel

RYB
color wheel

FIGURE 4.14 Complementary harmony in the key of Yellow. (Image created by Theresa-Marie Rhyne, 2016.)

4.5.3 Complementary Harmony

Complementary harmony represents colors that oppose or are across each other on the color wheel. In RGB/CMYK color space, the hue of Yellow is complementary to Blue. In the RYB color space, the hue of Yellow is complementary to Purple. In Figure 4.14, complementary harmony in the key hue of Yellow is depicted on both the RGB/CMYK and RYB color wheels.

4.5.3.1 Example of Complementary Harmony

We create a three-dimensional line chart of sales data over 4 months and apply a complementary harmony in the key of Yellow. In RGB/CMYK color space, Yellow opposes Blue on the color wheel and the two colors are complements. For our line chart example, we use tones of the Yellow and Blue hues for plotting our three-dimensional lines. These results are shown in Figure 4.15.

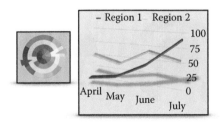

FIGURE 4.15 Example of complementary harmony. (Image created by Theresa-Marie Rhyne, 2016.)

4.5.4 Split Complementary Harmony

A *split complementary* harmony combines a key color with the two colors directly on either side of the complementary color. As we noted above, in RGB/CMYK color space, the hue of Yellow is complementary to Blue. So, the split complementary hues are Cyan Blue (Deep Sky Blue) and Blue Magenta (Purple). In the RYB color space, the hue of Yellow is complementary to Purple. The resulting split complementary hues are Blue Purple and Purple Red. In Figure 4.16, split complementary harmony in the key hue of Yellow is shown for the RGB/CMYK and RYB color wheels.

4.5.4.1 Example of Split Complementary Harmony
We build a two-dimensional bar chart with a line plot of sales data over 4 months and apply a split complementary harmony in the key of Yellow. To create a split complementary harmony, we use the colors on either side of Blue and combine them with Yellow. In RGB/CMYK color space, Yellow opposes Blue on the color wheel. The split complementary hues for Blue are Cyan Blue (Deep Sky Blue) and Blue Magenta (Purple). For our two-dimensional bar chart with a line plot example, we use shades and hues of Yellow with Cyan Blue and Blue Magenta (Purple) to form the split complementary harmony. These results are shown in Figure 4.17.

4.5.5 Analogous Complementary Harmony

The *analogous complementary* harmony represents a key color combined with its direct complement and the two colors on either side of the complement. As noted in the split complementary harmony discussion, in RGB/CMYK color space, the hue of Yellow is complementary to Blue and the split complementary hues are Cyan Blue (Deep Sky Blue) and Blue Magenta (Purple). So, the analogous complementary harmony in the key

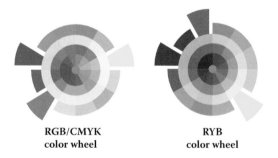

RGB/CMYK
color wheel

RYB
color wheel

FIGURE 4.16 Split complementary color harmony in the key of Yellow. (Image created by Theresa-Marie Rhyne, 2016.)

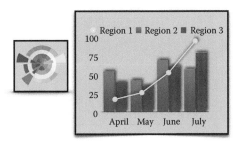

FIGURE 4.17 Example of split complementary harmony. (Image created by Theresa-Marie Rhyne, 2016.)

of Yellow combines Yellow with the three Blues that include Cyan Blue, Blue, and Blue Magenta. In the RYB color space, the hue of Yellow is complementary to Purple and the resulting split complementary hues are Blue Purple and Purple Red. The RYB analogous complementary harmony in the key of Yellow combines Yellow and the three Purples that encompass Blue Purple, Purple, and Purple Red. Figure 4.18 shows analogous complementary harmony in the key hue of Yellow for the RGB/CMYK and RYB color wheels.

4.5.5.1 Example of Analogous Complementary Harmony
In this example, a two-dimensional plot of sales data points for 3 months is shown with a trend line. We use an analogous complementary harmony in the key of Yellow for this plot. The trend line is shown with the Yellow hue. The hues with Blue at the center, Purple (Blue Magenta) to the left of Blue, and Cyan Blue to the right of Blue form the colors for the lines and the points of the 3 months of sales data. As the RGB/CMYK color wheel shows, this is an analogous complementary harmony. The Yellow hue is

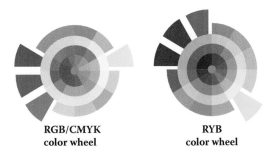

RGB/CMYK
color wheel

RYB
color wheel

FIGURE 4.18 Analogous complementary color harmony in the key of Yellow. (Image created by Theresa-Marie Rhyne, 2016.)

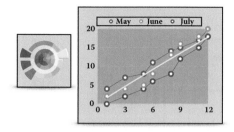

FIGURE 4.19 Example of analogous complementary harmony. (Image created by Theresa-Marie Rhyne, 2016.)

directly complementary to the three analogous colors of Purple, Blue, and Cyan Blue. Notice that the addition of a white center to the three hues of the points in the plot as well as the use of a darker gray background for the graph space changes the overall intensity of our four colors. This is an example of the concepts that Josef Albers wrote about in his book entitled *Interaction of Color* [6]. We discuss Josef Albers later in this chapter. These results are shown in Figure 4.19.

4.5.6 Double Complementary Harmony

The *double complementary* harmony includes two sets of complementary colors that are next to each other and across each other on the color wheel. For our example, we include the key hue of Yellow with its adjacent color of Orange in the RGB/CMYK color space. This results in Yellow and Orange combining with their respective complements of Blue and Cyan Blue (Deep Sky Blue). In RYB color space, we show the key hue of Yellow with its adjacent color of Orange Yellow. This results in Yellow and Orange Yellow combining with their respective complements of Purple and Blue Purple. The two complementary pairs crossing each other forms an X pattern on the color wheel. In Figure 4.20, double

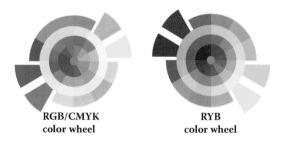

RGB/CMYK   RYB
color wheel   color wheel

FIGURE 4.20 Double complementary color harmony in the key of Yellow. (Image created by Theresa-Marie Rhyne, 2016.)

complementary harmony in the key hue of Yellow and adjacent Orange for the RGB/CMYK color wheel and double complementary harmony in the key hue of Yellow and adjacent Orange Yellow for the RYB color wheel are shown.

4.5.6.1 Example of Double Complementary Harmony
Here, we build a stacked two-dimensional bar chart for sales data during a 4-month timeframe. The stacked bar chart allows us to display the contribution of each of the four regions. For our colors, working in RGB/CMYK color space, we select a double complementary harmony in the key of Yellow. For our example, Yellow and Orange hues and tones are combined with respective hues and tones of their corresponding complements Blue and Cyan Blue. We show these results in Figure 4.21.

4.5.7 Tetrad Harmony
The *tetrad* harmony includes four hues that are equally distant from one another to form a rectangle or square on the color wheel. The result is two complementary pairs but spaced at least two steps apart for rectangular harmony and three steps apart for square harmony. We show an example of each in the key hue of yellow below.

4.5.7.1 Rectangular Harmony
With *rectangular* harmony, four hues are equally distant and form a rectangle on the color wheel. The result combines two pairs of complementary colors that are two steps apart on the color wheel. For our example, the key hue of Yellow and its Blue complement are two steps from Green and its Magenta complement on the RGB/CMYK color wheel while Yellow and its Purple complement are two steps from Green and its complement Red on the RYB color wheel. Figure 4.22 visually illustrates this concept.

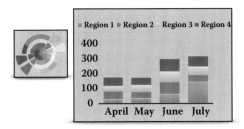

FIGURE 4.21   Example of double complementary harmony in the key of Yellow. (Image created by Theresa-Marie Rhyne, 2016.)

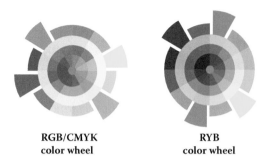

RGB/CMYK
color wheel   **RYB**
                              color wheel

FIGURE 4.22   Tetrad—rectangular color harmony in the key hue of Yellow. (Image created by Theresa-Marie Rhyne, 2016.)

4.5.7.1.1 Example of Tetrad–Rectangular Harmony

In this example, we work with a rectangular harmony in the key of Yellow to colorize a horizontal two-dimensional stacked bar chart of sales data in four regions over a timeframe of 4 months. To begin the rectangular harmony, we require two colors that are two steps from each other on the RGB/CMYK color wheel. Yellow and Green meet this requirement. The two complementary pairs of colors to define the rectangular harmony are Yellow and Blue with Green and Magenta. Using hues and shades of these four colors, we develop a horizontal stacked bar chart. Our results are shown in Figure 4.23.

4.5.7.2 Square Harmony

For *square* harmony, four colors are equidistant and three steps apart on the color wheel. Together, the four hues form a square on the color wheel that results in two pairs of complements. In Figure 4.24, Yellow and Blue complements combined with Green Cyan (Aqua Marine) and Magenta Red (Deep Pink) complements are shown on the RGB/CMYK color wheel

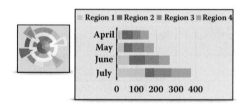

FIGURE 4.23   Example of tetrad—rectangular harmony in the key of Yellow. (Image created by Theresa-Marie Rhyne, 2016.)

along with Yellow and Purple complements combined with Green Blue and Red Orange on the RYB color wheel.

4.5.7.2.1 Example of Tetrad–Square Harmony

Here, we build an interactive two-dimensional bar chart of sales data in four regions over a timeframe of 4 months. With each time step (month), the values for each region change. We colorize this interactive information visualization example using a square harmony in the key of Yellow. For this square harmony, all four colors are equidistant and three steps apart on the RGB/CMYK color wheel. The resulting complementary pairs are Yellow and Blue with Green Cyan and Magenta Red. Using hues and tints of these four colors, we build the bar elements in this interactive example. Figure 4.25 shows a static image of time step 1 (April) of our results.

4.5.8 Diad Harmony

Diad harmony combines two colors that are two steps apart on the color wheel. Working again with our key hue of Yellow; the Yellow and Red

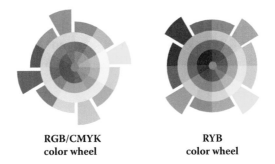

RGB/CMYK
color wheel

RYB
color wheel

FIGURE 4.24   Tetrad—square color harmony in the key hue of Yellow. (Image created by Theresa-Marie Rhyne, 2016.)

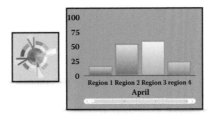

FIGURE 4.25   Example of tetrad—square harmony in the key of Yellow. (Image created by Theresa-Marie Rhyne, 2016.)

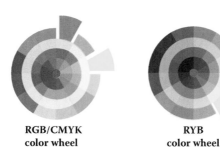

RGB/CMYK
color wheel　　　　　　**RYB**
　　　　　　　　　　　　　color wheel

FIGURE 4.26   Diad color harmony in the key hue of Yellow. (Image created by Theresa-Marie Rhyne, 2016.)

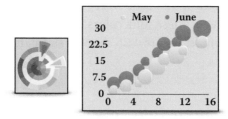

FIGURE 4.27   Example of diad harmony in the key of Yellow. (Image created by Theresa-Marie Rhyne, 2016.)

hues are two steps counter clockwise from each other on the RGB/CMYK color wheel. On the RYB color wheel, the Yellow and Orange hues are two steps counter clockwise from each other. Figure 4.26 shows these results for diad harmony.

4.5.8.1 Example of Diad Harmony

In this example, we develop a bubble chart of sales data for a 2-month timeframe. A diad color harmony is selected to depict the data values. We use Yellow as our key color and move two steps counter clockwise on the RGB/CMYK color wheel to select Red as our second color. Figure 4.27 depicts our results with Yellow and Red hues and tones applied to our bubble chart data.

4.5.9 Triad Harmony

Triad harmony includes three colors that are equally spaced from each other on the color wheel. The equal spacing creates an equilateral triangle on the wheel. Using the key hue of Yellow, the resulting triad includes the Cyan, Yellow, and Magenta colors on the RGB/CMYK color wheel. This combination encompasses the secondary colors of RGB color space or the primary colors of CMYK color space. On the RYB color wheel, the triad for the key hue of Yellow includes the RYB colors. This combination represents the primary colors of the RYB color space. Figure 4.28 shows these results for triad harmony.

4.5.9.1 Example of Triad Harmony

Here, we build an interactive bubble chart of sales data in three regions over a 12-month (1-year) timeframe. A triad color harmony in the key of Yellow is selected to colorize the data associated with the three regions. Our triad harmony includes three colors that are equally spaced from each other on the RGB/CMYK color wheel. With Yellow as the key, the other two colors are Cyan and Magenta. This combination is also both the set of secondary colors for the RGB color model and the set of primary colors for the CMYK color model. Figure 4.29 depicts our results for the last time step (December) in the interactive bubble chart with the pure hues of Yellow, Cyan, and Magenta applied to data.

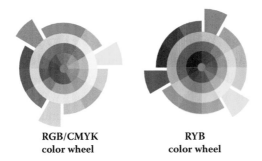

RGB/CMYK   RYB
color wheel   color wheel

FIGURE 4.28 Triad color harmony in the key hue of Yellow. (Image created by Theresa-Marie Rhyne, 2016.)

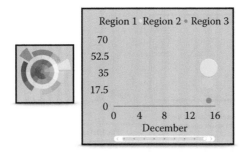

FIGURE 4.29 Example of triad harmony in the key of Yellow. (Image created by Theresa-Marie Rhyne, 2016.)

4.6 GAMUT MASKING FOR COLOR HARMONY

In Section 4.5, we presented many types of color harmony. One challenge many designers and painters confront revolves around narrowing down the color wheel possibilities to only focus on a specific group of colors when creating or building color content. *Gamut masking* is an approach for defining a specific range of colors or a color harmony grouping on the color wheel. In 2010, James Gurney, a highly regarded author and illustrator of the Dinotopia series, outlined his approach to what he called "Color Wheel or Gamut Masking" in his book on *Color and Light: A Guide for the Realist Painter* [7]. Gurney showed how one could cut out, or mask, only portions of the color wheel that were desired for a given color scheme. This allowed for focusing on a subset of the color wheel in developing the color palette for a given painting. Richard Robinson, using Flash, built an online tool entitled *Gamut Masking* inspired from Gurney's writings [8,9]. Robinson's tool provides either the RYB color wheel for painters or the RGB/CMYK color wheel for photographers, printers, and digital content developers to facilitate the color wheel masking process. Robinson defines the RYB color wheel as the *Standard* wheel and the RGB/CMYK color wheel as the *Yurmby* (Yellow Red Magenta Blue Cyan Green) color wheel. Each color wheel also spins colors around for more interactive exploration of color harmony. Robinson's tool, endorsed by James Gurney, is available under Robinson's "Live Painting Lessons" web site at http://www .livepaintinglessons.com/gamutmask.php. The Gamut Mask Tool is Flash based and requires the Flash plug-in from Adobe that is available at http:// www.adobe.com/products/flashplayer.html. As a result, a laptop or desktop computing environment is usually needed to run the Gamut Mask Tool.

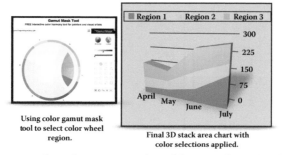

FIGURE 4.30 Using the color gamut mask tool for an infographic design. (Image created by Theresa-Marie Rhyne, 2016, using the Color *Gamut Mask* tool, http:// www.livepaintinglessons.com/gamutmask.php.)

In Figure 4.30, we use the color gamut mask tool with the Yurmby (RGB/CMYK) color wheel option to develop a three-dimensional stacked area chart. The sample data set of sales over a 4-month period used in Section 4.5 is used to generate the numeric values for the infographic or information visualization. We apply the cool colors concept noted in Section 4.4 and develop a mask for the analogous colors of Green Cyan, Cyan, and Cyan Blue. Our color gamut mask also provides us a sense of how color quantities will appear when we apply the analogous colors of Green Cyan, Cyan, and Cyan Blue to our stacked area chart.

4.7 REVISITING THE HISTORICAL EVOLUTION OF THE COLOR WHEEL AND COLOR HARMONY

Now that we have discussed the construction of color wheels and defined color harmony, we can revisit the historical evolution of the color wheel. There were and are many contributors to color theory over the centuries in the Western World. We highlight a select few who helped define concepts pertaining to the evolution of the color wheel and color harmony. For a more robust discussion of the history of color theory in the Western World, we refer you to Rolf G. Kuehni's 2003 book on *Color Space and Its Divisions: Color Order from Antiquity to the Present* [10]. In the References section, we also list original source materials as further readings about the contributions to color harmony we will describe in this section.

4.7.1 Revisiting Isaac Newton's Color Circle

As we noted in Chapter 1, Isaac Newton developed the initial concept of the color circle or the color wheel and published it in his 1704 book, entitled *Opticks* [11]. Newton's color wheel was based on depicting colors in the spectrum of light in a closed circle. Figure 1.8 shows Newton's color circle diagram. Newton's diagram was fundamental in its geometry but did not include color relationships as a concept.

4.7.2 Revisiting Moses Harris' Color Wheels

In 1766, over 60 years after Isaac Newton's writings on the color circle, Moses Harris further evolved the color wheel in his *Natural System of Colours* book [12]. Harris made the first known published attempt to diagram the RYB color wheel. He defined a *prismatic* or primary color wheel for RYB as well as a *compound* color wheel for the secondary colors of Orange, Green, and Purple. Harris' color wheels are shown in Figure 1.9 and included 18 divisions on the wheel. Following similar steps to what we defined in Section 4.2.3, Harris included the primary RYB colors; the secondary RYB colors of Orange, Green, and Purple; and the tertiary colors that mix a primary and secondary color on his prismatic color wheel. Harris chose a finer level of detail for the tertiary colors. Harris noted, for example, that Orange Red was a different color from Red Orange as we move clockwise from Red at the top of his color wheel. He did not specifically develop complementary color relationships. Harris' work functioned as an inventory of hues, tones, and shades of color similar to concepts we noted in Section 4.3.

4.7.3 Revisiting Johann Wolfgang von Goethe's Color Wheel

In his 1810 *Theory of Colours* publication, Johann Wolfgang von Goethe defined the color wheel in a format similar to what we are familiar with today [13]. Goethe developed a symmetric color wheel composed of colors that oppose or complement each other where complementary colors cancel each other out to produce Gray or Black when mixed as pigments. Figure 1.10 shows Goethe's concept that is similar to our discussions on the first two steps in constructing a color wheel in Section 4.2. As we noted in Section 1.4, another significant contribution that Goethe made was to include Magenta as a color in his color theories. Magenta is not a spectral color such as those we noted in Section 2.1. However, it is a color we, as humans, mentally see in after images produced by our brain. Magenta is also a primary color of the printing process. Goethe's addition of Magenta or Red Purple also provided an effective closure to the color wheel between Purple and Red and thus has remained on color wheels to this day.

4.7.4 Examining Philipp Otto Runge's Color Sphere

Philipp Otto Runge, a contemporary of Goethe, developed and published one of the first recognized three-dimensional sphere models in color theory [14]. Runge defined the complete space of color as consisting of the RYB chromatic primaries, Black and White achromatic primaries, and their mixtures. He built a color circle with RYB forming the primaries as well as Orange, Green, and Purple forming the secondary colors on the color wheel as we have shown in Figure 4.3. He conceived of a color sphere with White forming the top and Black forming the bottom opposing poles of the sphere. Runge published his color sphere concept in a manuscript entitled *Die Farben-Kugel* (*The Color Sphere*) in 1810 and unfortunately died shortly thereafter [15]. Goethe later published key letters

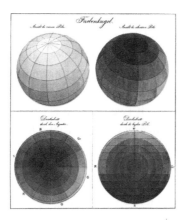

FIGURE 4.31 Philipp Otto Runge's color sphere hand-painted illustration. (From Runge, P. O., *Die Farben-Kugel (Color Sphere), oder Construction des Verhaeltnisses aller Farben zueinander,* Hamburg, Perthes, 1810; Stahl, G. (trans.), *On Vision and Colors by Arthur Schopenhauer and Color Sphere by Philipp Otto Runge,* Princeton Architectural Press, New York, NY, 2010, public domain.)

from Runge in Goethe's own publications. Runge used the color sphere to define pleasing or discordant color combinations, thus developing color harmony concepts. Many contributors to color theory built upon Runge's work. These individuals include Albert Munsell and Johannes Itten. As we noted in Section 3.6, Albert Munsell revitalized the color sphere concept in Munsell's early efforts to develop a color notation system. However, Munsell soon discovered that color space was not naturally geometrically regular. Munsell abandoned the color sphere concept to build his color system on equally perceived color differences that produced branching geometry called a color tree, shown Figure 3.12. Later in this section, we will discuss the contributions of Johannes Itten and his colleagues at the Bauhaus in the 1920s to color harmony and art education. Figure 4.31 shows Runge's initial color sphere concept that he hand drew for his 1810 *The Color Sphere* publication [16].

4.7.5 Revisiting Michel Chevreul's Color Wheel

As noted in Chapter 1, Michel Chevreul further emphasized complementary colors on the color wheel to support his color contrasts concepts that appeared in his 1839 book *The Principles of Harmony and Contrast of Colours, and their Application to the Arts* [17]. Figure 1.12 depicts the color wheel Chevreul developed. Chevreul actually defined a hemispherical color model to predict his contrast effects where the color wheel is the bottom cross section of the hemisphere. Following similar steps to what we noted in Section 4.2.3, Chevreul located the RYB primaries and the Orange, Green, and Purple secondary colors at equal sixths around the circumference of his color wheel. The tertiary colors were added between the primary and secondary colors. Chevreul added finer divisions to his color wheel by dividing each twelfth into six intervals for a wheel of 22 hues. Chevreul also specifically ensured that a hue and its direct complement opposed each other on his color wheel to emphasize his color harmony and contrasts concepts.

4.7.6 Exploring George Field's Color Wheel

In a similar time frame, George Field, trained as a chemist, manufactured and sold paint colors for artists in Great Britain. Field experimented with various production methods of color pigments and his products were well regarded among professional artists. In 1817, he published *Chromatics or, an Essay on the Analogy and Harmony of Colours* that outlined color harmony concepts for the RYB color model [18]. His 1835 publication on the *Chromatography; or, a Treatise on Colours and Pigments, and of their Powers in Painting* presented practical concepts about color that encompassed pigments as well as drying, and preserving products [19,20]. His second book became a key reference on color for painters and other artists. From his extensive testing efforts, Field offered detailed observations of close to all of the commercially available pigments at the time of publication of his writing. He thus provided a reliable handbook and the framework for revisions to the book that aided artists for years to come. Field provided detailed discussions of tertiary colors, the combinations of primary and secondary colors, and developed a detailed color wheel of pigment mixtures. Field's terminology and diagram is still widely regarded today in terms of RYB color pigment mixing and color harmony. Field also included a chapter on *new optical instruments* with light and color experiments noted. Many of Field's notions on light and color from the RYB color model perspective, however, were proven to be in error with James Clerk Maxwell's 1861 demonstration of the RGB color model that we highlighted in Section 1.1 [21]. Figure 4.32 shows George Field's color wheel from his *Chromatography; or, a Treatise on Colours and Pigments, and of their Powers in Painting* book. The hand-painted Red and Blue hues have faded with time but the labeling still remains.

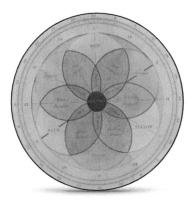

FIGURE 4.32 George Field's Color Wheel illustration. (From Field, G., *Chromatography: Or, a Treatise on Colours and Pigments, and of Their Powers in Painting*, Charles Tilt, Fleet Street, London, 1835, public domain.)

4.7.7 Examining Ogden N. Rood's *Modern Chromatics* Writings

In 1879, Ogden N. Rood published his book on *Modern Chromatics, with Applications to Art and Industry* [22]. The book was also translated into German in 1880 and French in 1881. Rood was a professor of Physics at Columbia University and an amateur painter. His book presented trichromatic color vision concepts with a focus on Thomas Young's work, defined color harmony, discussed color contrasts, and addressed mixing of pigment paints in detail. He presented many of the color concepts that Newton, Goethe, Chevreul, Field, and others had developed in a format that was understandable to a *layperson* and appealed to artists. Rood also developed an early Hue, Saturation, and Brightness model similar to the Hue, Saturation, and Value concepts we have presented in Section 3.7. In an appendix, the *Modern Chromatics* book also mentioned Hering's opponent color theory notions. Rood's book was credited as being hugely influential to Impressionist and Neo-Impressionist artists of the time. George Seurat's pointillism painting style was influenced by readings of Rood's discussion on the theory of contrasting colors [23]. We show illustrations from Rood's *Modern Chromatics* book in Figure 4.33.

4.7.8 Examining Color Wheel Instruction Writings by Louis Prang and Milton Bradley

Although Rood described the RGB color model and the resulting RGB color wheel in a format that artists could understand; many practicing artists

Front plate of Rood's *Modern Chromatics* book:
published in 1879

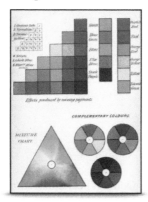

FIGURE 4.33   Front plate illustration from Ogden N. Rood's *Modern Chromatics*. (From Rood, O.N., *Modern Chromatics, with Applications to Art and Industry*, D. Appleton and Company, New York, NY, 1879, public domain.)

and art educators continued to use the RYB color model when it came to discussing color pigments and color harmony. In 1893, Louis Prang, Mary Dana Hicks, and John S. Clark published the book, *Instruction in Color for Public Schools,* and defined a color wheel similar to the RYB Color Wheel that we have shown in Figure 4.3 [24]. This color wheel is frequently called the Prang color wheel after Louis Prang who described it and color harmony concepts for art education purposes. Interestingly, Louis Prang is also known as the *father* of the American Christmas card. In the 1890s, Milton Bradley, the founder of the Milton Bradley Company known for creating board games, published several books on color instruction at the primary and secondary school levels. His book on *Elementary Color* provided guidelines for teaching color pigments mixing and color harmony with the RYB color model [25]. As a result of these and other contributions, the RYB color wheel and color harmony concepts became fundamental to kindergarten and elementary school education.

4.7.9 Exploring Bauhaus Contributions to Color Harmony and Interaction

From 1919 to 1933, an art school in Germany operated that combined a unique approach to design with crafts and fine arts. The Bauhaus school was founded on the basis of creating a *total* work of art in which all arts could be brought together. This concept encompassed textiles, painting, sculpture, graphic design, interior design, architecture, industrial design, and typography as well as other design disciplines. Color theory was a basic part of the curriculum and included in the first-year preliminary course, among others. Several Bauhaus instructors rotated teaching the preliminary course as well as expressing their notions of color theory in other classes. We review key concepts introduced by four Bauhaus instructors who highlighted color: Paul Klee, Wassily Kandinsky, Johannes Itten, and Josef Albers. Each of these instructors interacted with one another while at the Bauhaus, and it is possible to observe some blending of their concepts. Each artist, however, maintained his own unique approach to presenting color fundamentals via the RYB color model and wheel in their teachings and individual art compositions.

4.7.9.1 Paul Klee's Teachings of Color

Paul Klee discussed differences between the visual perception of color pigments and the nature of color as light. Klee also highlighted how colors are altered with changes in the purity or intensity of a color (saturation) as well as changes in the lightness or darkness of a color (value). We featured some of these changes previously in Figure 4.4. In his teachings of color, Klee highlighted the relationship between hue, chroma (also termed colorfulness), and value using the color wheel that was at the equator of a color sphere similar to Philipp Otto Runge's sphere noted in Figure 4.31. Klee produced detailed notebooks on his lectures that are available today in multimedia format as the *Notebooks of Paul Klee, Volumes 1 & 2*. We list these writings in the References section at the end of this chapter [26,27].

4.7.9.2 Wassily Kandinsky's Teachings of Color

Wassily Kandinsky taught Bauhaus students about the notion that color itself, not necessarily the object colored, evokes a perceptual response. As a result, the juxtaposition of line and color can result in a sense of movement. Figures 4.15 and 4.19 are two examples of implementations of this concept. Prior to his arrival at the Bauhaus in 1922, Kandinsky released a significant treatise entitled *Concerning the Spiritual in Art* in 1910 that was translated from German into English in 1911 [5]. In this essay, Kandinsky advanced the concepts of abstract art by expressing his belief that color could be used in a painting independent of the visual description of an object or scene. At the Bauhaus, Kandinsky taught the preliminary course where he further evolved color concepts beyond the warm and cool concepts that we noted in Section 4.4.

4.7.9.3 Johannes Itten's Teachings of Color

Johannes Itten pioneered the teaching of the preliminary course at the Bauhaus in 1919. Itten used the RYB 12-sectioned color wheel of primary, secondary, and tertiary colors similar to what we have diagrammed in Figure 4.3. His teachings highlighted color harmony and color contrasts. Like Klee and as previously noted, Itten also defined a color sphere concept that extended the concepts of Philipp Otto Runge. A two-dimensional cross section of Itten's color sphere, based on the RYB color model, is frequently called a *color star*. Many of his color theory concepts appeared in a book he later (1961) published in German entitled *The Art of Color: The Subjective Experience and Objective Rationale of Color*. After Itten's death in 1967, Faber Birren published a condensed and simplified version of Itten's original writings and entitled it *The Elements of Color: A Treatise on the Color System of Johannes Itten Based on His Book 'The Art of Color.'* Birren's condensed version was officially published in 1970. These references are cited in the References section of this chapter. Itten's discussions of the RYB color model and color harmony concepts are still used to introduce students to color today [28,29].

4.7.9.4 Josef Albers' Teachings of Color

Josef Albers' teachings focused on the concept that the perception of color is always relative and subjective. Albers developed student exercises that demonstrated how color deceives continually. In Figure 4.19, Albers' concepts are illustrated where the addition of a solid White circle inside the Cyan, Blue, and Purple data points creates a three-dimensional, vibrating affect. In Figure 4.21, although a two-dimensional bar chart is shown, the Yellow, Orange, Blue, and Cyan Blue rectangles when combined together create a three-dimensional perception. Albers' teachings and exercises emphasized that applying rules of color harmony does not always address color interactions and deceptions. Josef Albers originally came to the Bauhaus as a student from 1920 to 1923, enrolling in the preliminary course taught by Itten and attending glass-painting workshops. In 1923, he was appointed to the teaching staff and given a commission to teach the preliminary course. From 1925 until the Bauhaus' closure in 1933, Albers served as either the codirector or director of the preliminary course. During this time frame, Albers began to develop many of his notions about color being the primary medium of pictorial language. Albers met and married Anni Albers, who went on to pioneer in textile arts, during the Bauhaus years. After the closure of the

Bauhaus, the husband and wife team immigrated to the United States and taught at Black Mountain College in Asheville, North Carolina. The couple left Black Mountain and eventually moved on to Yale University in 1950, where Josef Albers led and taught in the Department of Design until his retirement in 1958. They remained at Yale University until their respective deaths. Many of Josef Albers' students, such as Kenneth Nolan, pioneered abstract painting movements such as *color field painting* [30,31].

From 1949 until his death in 1976, Josef Albers explored colors and chromatic interactions with nested squares in his paintings and prints, entitled collectively *Homage to a Square*. In 1963, he published the book *Interaction of Color*. The book was conceived as a handbook and teaching aid to explain complex color theory principles to artists, instructors, and students. The original version, published by Yale University Press, was a limited silk-screen edition with 150 color plates. In 1971, a paperback version that featured 10 color studies chosen by Albers was released and continues to remain in print. Albers' landmark book includes case studies and exercises on (1) color relativity, intensity, and temperature; (2) color contrasts such as vibrating and vanishing boundaries; and (3) optical illusions of transparency and reversed grounds. His intent was not to develop a set of color harmony rules or guidelines. Rather, Albers designed his book to be a set of opportunities to discover and explore the magic of color. The *Interaction of Color* is considered to be one of the most comprehensive examinations of the function and perception of color to this day. The book profoundly influenced art education and art practice in the twentieth century and continues to do so today. Reference [6] provides a specific citation of the 50th anniversary edition of this book.

4.8 MODERNIZING ALBERS' INTERACTION OF COLOR STUDIES WITH AN APP

In 2013, the 50th anniversary editions of the *Interaction of Color* book were released as well as a mobile iPad app for interactively working with the digital book's exercises. The app was designed and implemented by Potion Design Studio under the direction of Yale University Press and the Josef & Anni Albers Foundation. The *Interaction of Color by Josef Albers* mobile app is available for purchase from the iTunes store and is priced at $13.99 [32–34]. The app was designed to be a near-digital replica of the 1963 version of *the Interaction of Color* book, including the implementation of the original Baskerville typeface and layout of the

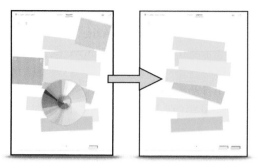

Construction of Yellow color   Completed Yellow color intensity
intensity study using interaction   study using interacion of color
of color ipad app.   ipad app.

FIGURE 4.34 Creating an intensity color study in the key of Yellow with the *Interaction of Color by Josef Albers* iPad App. We use a template from the *Interaction of Color* App for the iPad (http://yupnet.org/interactionofcolor/), copyrighted by Yale University Press, to create a color intensity study in the key of Yellow. (Image created by Theresa-Marie Rhyne, 2016, using the *Interaction of Color* App templates. With permission from Yale University Press.)

text columns with twenty-first century upgrades such as an interactive color wheel. The iPad app includes digital versions of the color exercises with the corresponding written discussions of the exercises from the original book. The exercises can be used and saved for creating personal color studies and applications. In Figure 4.34, we work with an intensity color study in the key of Yellow, created with one of the *Interaction of Color* iPad app templates.

4.9 CONCLUDING REMARKS

In this chapter, we reviewed the color wheel for the respective RGB, CMYK, and RYB color models. We showed hues, tints, tones, and shades on the color wheel. Next, we defined color harmony as the process of choosing colors, from the color wheel, that work well together in the composition of an image. Nine types of color harmony with an example for each were presented: (1) monochromatic, (2) analogous, (3) complementary, (4) split complementary, (5) analogous complementary, (6) double complementary, (7) tetrad—rectangular and square, (8) diad, and (9) triad. We also revisited the historical evolution of the color wheel and color harmony, building on our preliminary review in Section 1.4. In Chapter 5, we will discuss further online and mobile apps that aid in creating color content and assist in analyzing the color harmony or scheme of an existing digital image.

REFERENCES

1. Eldridge, K. (2008). *The Complete Color Harmony Workbook*. Gloucester, MA: Rockport Publishers.
2. Smith, K. (2016). Sensational Color. Available at http://www.sensational -color.com/, accessed January 15, 2016.
3. Tiger Color. (2016). Color Harmonies. Available at http://www.tigercolor .com/color-lab/color-theory/color-harmonies.htm, accessed January 15, 2016.
4. Briggs, D. (2013). Part 7: The Dimension of Hue, The Dimensions of Color. Available at http://www.huevaluechroma.com/071.php, accessed January 27, 2016.
5. Kandinsky, W. and Sadler, M.T.H. (2008). *Concerning the Spiritual in Art*. Auckland, New Zealand: The Floating Press (first published in 1911). Available at https://books.google.com/books?id=03ugtxqGZYMC&printse c=frontcover&source=gbs_ge_summary_r&cad=0#v=onepage&q&f=false
6. Albers, J. (2013). *Interaction of Color*, 50th Anniversary Edition. New Haven, CT: Yale University Press.
7. Gurney, J. (2010). *Color and Light: A Guide for the Realist Painter*. Kansas City, MO: Andrews McMeel Publishing.
8. Gurney, J. (2011). Part3: Gamut Masking Method, Gurney Journey. Available at http://gurneyjourney.blogspot.com/2011/09/part-3-gamut -masking-method.html
9. Robinson, R. (2010). Gamut Mask Tool, Live Painting Lessons. Available at http://www.livepaintinglessons.com/gamutmask.php
10. Kuehni, R.G. (2003). *Color Space and Its Divisions: Color Order from Antiquity to the Present*. Hoboken, NJ: John Wiley & Sons.
11. Newton, I. (1704). *Opticks: or, a Treatise of the Reflexions, Refractions, Inflexions and Colours of Light. Also Two Treatises of the Species and Magnituder of Curvilinear Figures*. London, United Kingdom: Samuel Smith and Benjamin Walford. Available from The Project Gutenberg EBook of Opticks at http://www.gutenberg.org/files/33504/33504-h/33504-h.htm, accessed December 09, 2015.
12. Harris, M. (1766). *The Natural System of Colors*. Leicester-Fields, England: Laidler.
13. von Goethe, J.W. (1840). *Goethe's Theory of Colours*, Translated with notes by C.L. Eastlake R.A. F.R.S. London, United Kingdom: John Murray. Available at https://archive.org/details/goethestheoryco01goetgoog
14. Kuehni, R.G. (2008). Philipp Otto Runge's Color Sphere: A Translation with Related Materials and an Essay. Available at http://www.iscc.org/pdf /RungeFarben-Kugel.pdf and Inter-Society Color Council, http://www.iscc. org/.
15. Runge, P.O. (1810). *Die Farben-Kugel (Color Sphere), oder Construction des Verhaeltnisses aller Farben zueinander*. Hamburg: Perthes.
16. Stahl, G. (trans.) (2010). *On Vision and Colors by Arthur Schopenhauer and Color Sphere by Philipp Otto Runge*. New York, NY: Princeton Architectural Press.

17. Chevreul, M.E. (1839). *De la loi du contraste simultané des couleurs et de l'assortiment des objets colorés*, Translated by C. Martel as *The Principles of Harmony and Contrast of Colours*. London, UK: Longman, Brown, Green and Longmans.
18. Field, G. (1817). *Chromatics: An Essay on the Analogy and Harmony of Colours*. London: A.J. Valpy, Tookes Court, Chancery Lane.
19. Field, G. (1835). *Chromatography: or, a Treatise on Colours and Pigments, and of their Powers in Painting*. London: Charles Tilt, Fleet Street.
20. Shires, L.M. (2016). On Color Theory, 1835: George Field's Chromatography. BRANCH: Britain, Representation and Nineteenth-Century History. In D.F. Felluga (ed.), *Extension of Romanticism and Victorianism on the Net*. Available at http://www.branchcollective.org/?ps_articles=linda-m-shires-on-color-theory-1835-george-fields-chromatography.
21. British Journal of Photography. (1861). The Theory of the Primary Colors. Available at http://notesonphotographs.org/index.php?title=%22The_Theory_of_the_Primary_Colours.%22_The_British_Journal_of_Photography,_August_9,_1861
22. Rood, O.N. (1879. *Modern Chromatics, with Applications to Art and Industry*. New York, NY: Appleton and Company.
23. Russell, J. (1965). *Seurat*. London, United Kingdom: Thames and Hudson.
24. Prang, L., Hicks, M.D., and Clark, J.S. (1893). *Suggestions for a Course of Instruction in Color for Public Schools*. New York, NY: The Prang Educational Company.
25. Bradley, M. (1895). *Elementary Color*, Third Edition. Springfield, MA: Milton Bradley Company.
26. Klee, P. and Spiller, J. (2014). *The Notebooks of Paul Klee, Volume 1: The Thinking Eye*. San Francisco, CA: Wittenborn Art Books (Multimedia CD).
27. Klee, P. and Spiller, J. (2014). *The Notebooks of Paul Klee, Volume 2: The Nature of Nature*. San Francisco, CA: Wittenborn Art Books (Multimedia CD).
28. Itten, J. (1974). *The Art of Color: The Subjective Experience and Objective Rationale of Color*. Hoboken, NJ: John Wiley & Sons.
29. Itten, J. and Birren, F. (1970). *The Elements of Color: A Treatise on the Color System of Johannes Itten Based on His Book The Art of Color*. Hoboken, NJ: John Wiley & Sons.
30. The Art Story. (2016). Color Field Painting. Available at http://www.theartstory.org/movement-color-field-painting.htm
31. The Art Story. (2016). Kenneth Noland. Available at http://www.theartstory.org/artist-noland-kenneth.htm
32. Yale University Press. (2016). Interaction of Color App for iPad. Available at http://yupnet.org/interactionofcolor/
33. Potion Design Studio. (2016). Interaction of Color, Yale University Press, Mobile App. Available at http://www.potiondesign.com/project/interaction-of-color/
34. The Josef & Anni Albers Foundation. (2016). Biographies. Available at http://www.albersfoundation.org/artists/biographies/

CHAPTER 5

Analyzing and Modifying with Online and Mobile Color Tools

5.1 OVERVIEW OF ONLINE AND MOBILE COLOR TOOLS

There are many online and mobile color tools to aid the process of color scheme design and selection. We have learned the fundamentals of color vision in Chapter 2, principles of color systems in Chapter 3, and the language of color harmony in Chapter 4, and we now examine how some of these color applications work. A number of online tools such as Paletton Color Scheme Designer and ColorBrewer offer color scheme suggestions. Some online and mobile apps import a digital image of a scene or visualization and evaluate the existing color palette of the image. The Adobe Capture CC and Color Companion mobile apps support this capability. Adobe Color CC allows for digital image import as well as creating a color scheme directly from the Red, Green, and Blue (RGB)/Cyan, Magenta, Yellow, and Key Black (CMYK) color wheel. A few mobile apps automatically match colors in a digital image to an existing library of color values. The PANTONE Studio app works in this manner by matching hues to the Pantone color library. Other color tools provide minimal automated color suggestion and prefer to allow the users to individually select or navigate the desired colors of choice in the imported image. The COLOURlovers' COPASO online application works in this way. The *Interaction of Color by Josef Albers* app for the iPad is more of a discovery of color behavior app that can also assist in the design selection process. This chapter highlights eight online or mobile color tools to help navigate through the process of color evaluation, suggestion, and application. These tools are as follows: (1) Adobe Color CC, (2) Adobe Capture CC, (3) the COLOURlovers community and its Color Palette Software (COPASO) tool, (4) Paletton's Color Scheme Designer, (5) Color Companion, (6) PANTONE Studio, (7) ColorBrewer 2.0, and (8) the *Interaction of Color by Josef Albers* iPad app.

5.2 ADOBE COLOR CC

Adobe Color, previously called Adobe Kuler, is an online or Internet application from Adobe Systems. It allows for testing, creating, and saving color schemes that consist of five colors. Central to the Adobe Color application is a RGB/CMYK color wheel and supporting color harmony options of analogous, monochromatic, triad, complementary, compound, shades, and custom. We covered most of these color harmony types in Chapter 4. Additionally, the application allows for importing a jpeg image and automatically selects the key colors in the image. Adobe Color also provides the ability to explore the colors in the imported image, creating your own customized palette of five colors. The online Adobe Color application can be freely experimented with at https://color.adobe.com. An Adobe ID is required to: (1) save color schemes for future use, (2) access and share an inventory of color themes created by other members of the Adobe Color community, and (3) integrate Adobe Color palettes with other Adobe Creative Cloud software services such as Adobe Photoshop or Adobe Illustrator. An Adobe ID is free to setup and can be done by going to https://accounts.adobe.com. See References [1,2] for additional information on the use of Adobe Color CC. We work through two examples, which are shown in Sections 5.2.1 and 5.2.2, using Adobe Color. Figure 5.1 shows the Adobe Color CC user interface with the color palette from a captured image, which will be highlighted in our second example below.

5.2.1 Creating Color Schemes with the Adobe Color Wheel

In this first example with Adobe Color, we used the provided RGB/CMYK color wheel to select two color harmonies of analogous and triad in the key of Purple. We covered the concepts of the color wheel and color harmony previously in Chapter 4. Adobe Color allows us to select our key or *base color* and from there provides color harmony options. The detail of the Adobe Color user interface is shown in Figure 5.2.

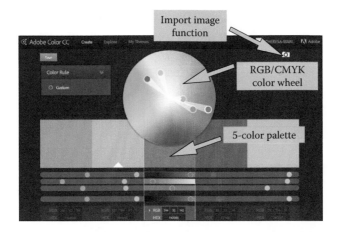

FIGURE 5.1   User interface to the Adobe Color CC tool (https://color.adobe.com). (Image created by Theresa-Marie Rhyne, 2016, using the Adobe Color tool.)

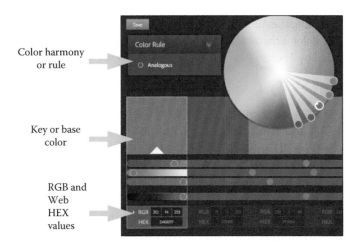

FIGURE 5.2   Detail of the Adobe Color CC user interface (https://color.adobe .com). (Image created by Theresa-Marie Rhyne, 2016, using the Adobe Color tool.)

We used the sample data set of sales over a 4-month period applied to color harmony examples in Chapter 4 to build an infographic or information visualization. We decided to build a three-dimensional stacked bar chart, created with Apple Numbers and Pages software. Therefore, we require three different color values to depict the differences in sales between three regions. As noted previously, Adobe Color provides color

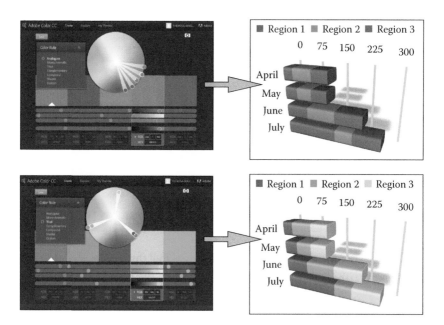

FIGURE 5.3   Using the Adobe Color CC tool (https://color.adobe.com) to develop two possible color schemes for a three-dimensional (3D) stacked bar chart. (Image created by Theresa-Marie Rhyne, 2016, using the Adobe Color CC tool.)

harmonies or rules options to aid in creating a color scheme. We selected the analogous and triad rules or harmonies for the key or base color of Purple as options. The results are shown in Figure 5.3.

5.2.2 Capturing a Color Scheme from an Image with Adobe Color

In our second example with Adobe Color, we import a jpeg image into Adobe Color to analyze the colors in the image. Our jpeg image is entitled *Spring Garden* and was the same image used in Section 3.9.4 as part of our discussion on Web color selection. As we noted in Section 2.9, "jpeg" stands for the Joint Photographic Experts Group and is a frequently used compression format for digital images. In Figure 5.4, the work-flow diagram for capturing colors in the image is shown. In Step 1, the jpeg image of *Spring Garden* is imported and Adobe Color automatically creates a color scheme based on a statistical analysis of the top five colors of the image. The selected five colors are displayed as moveable circle sensors on the image. In Step 2, the user can modify the proposed color scheme by moving the five color sensors to create a desired color palette. In Step 3, the

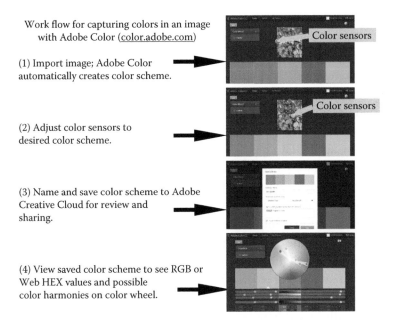

Work flow for capturing colors in an image with Adobe Color (color.adobe.com)

Color sensors

(1) Import image; Adobe Color automatically creates color scheme.

Color sensors

(2) Adjust color sensors to desired color scheme.

(3) Name and save color scheme to Adobe Creative Cloud for review and sharing.

(4) View saved color scheme to see RGB or Web HEX values and possible color harmonies on color wheel.

FIGURE 5.4 Workflow depicting the use of the Adobe Color tool (https://color .adobe.com) to capture a color scheme from an image. (Image created by Theresa-Marie Rhyne, 2016, using the Adobe Color CC tool.)

user, with an Adobe ID, names and saves the color scheme to their Adobe Creative Cloud space for review and sharing. For our example, the color scheme is named *Spring Garden*. In Step 4, when the saved *Spring Garden* color scheme is retrieved, the RGB and Web HEX values are displayed. A RGB/CMYK color wheel also displays potential color harmonies of the saved color scheme. For our *Spring Garden* color scheme, the Magenta and Green hues are nearly opposing each other on the color wheel. As we learned in Section 4.5.3, two colors opposing each other on the color wheel form a complementary color harmony. Therefore, our *Spring Garden* color scheme approximates a complementary color harmony.

5.3 ADOBE CAPTURE CC

The *Adobe Capture CC* app, available for free on Android and iOS platforms, allows capturing colors from photos on your mobile device. Adobe provides more information at http://www.adobe.com/products /capture.html. As noted in the previous discussion on Adobe Color CC in Section 5.2, a free Adobe ID is required to use Adobe Capture CC and can be obtained at https://accounts.adobe.com. Adobe Capture

CC easily imports images from your mobile device's camera or photo library. The app automatically creates a color palette of five key colors in the image. The five key colors are noted with color sensors that are moveable circles on the imported image. The user can create a custom palette of desired colors by moving the color sensors around on the imported image. References [3,4] highlight additional features of the mobile app. Figure 5.5 shows the user interface for capturing color in the Adobe Capture CC app.

The desired color palette or scheme can be saved to your Adobe Cloud space for future use. The Web HEX and RGB values of the color scheme can be found by editing the saved color palette. Adobe color palettes are also easily integrated into other Adobe tools such as Illustrator CC or Photoshop CC on the desktop and Illustrator Draw and Photoshop Sketch on mobile devices. Figure 5.6 shows the steps for using the Adobe Capture CC app to create a color palette from a digital photo captured or stored on your mobile device.

We have discussed how saved color palettes from image-capture work can be stored for future use. Figure 5.7 shows the application of our *Spring Garden* color palette to a pie chart infographic.

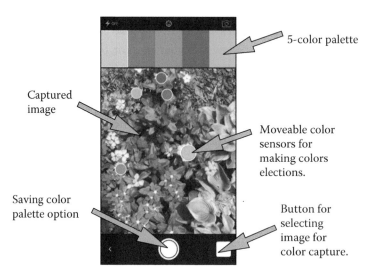

FIGURE 5.5 User interface to the Adobe Capture CC for capturing color from an image (http://www.adobe.com/products/capture.html). (Image created by Theresa-Marie Rhyne, 2016, using the Adobe Capture app.)

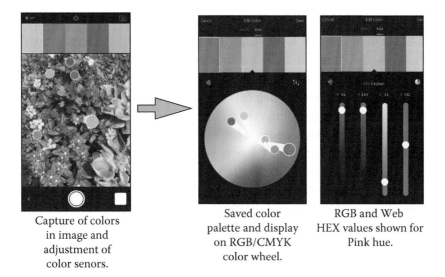

| Capture of colors in image and adjustment of color senors. | Saved color palette and display on RGB/CMYK color wheel. | RGB and Web HEX values shown for Pink hue. |

FIGURE 5.6 Using the Adobe Capture CC app to capture the colors in a *Spring Garden* photo located on an iPhone. (Image created by Theresa-Marie Rhyne, 2016, using the Adobe Capture app, http://www.adobe.com/products/capture.html.)

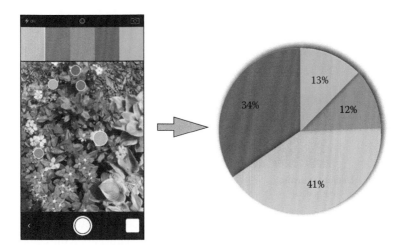

FIGURE 5.7 Applying the *Spring Garden* color scheme to the development of a pie chart infographic. (Image created by Theresa-Marie Rhyne, 2016, using the Adobe Capture app, http://www.adobe.com/products/capture.html.)

5.4 COLOURLOVERS' COMMUNITY

COLOURlovers.com is free social network service that focuses on (1) developing a library of color palettes and patterns created by its user community, (2) discussing color trends in various arenas that apply color, and (3) providing free and helpful online and app tools for color discovery and analysis. A user joins the COLOURlover's community by registering and opening an account at https://www.colourlovers.com/register. The site indicates that there are over six million colors and two million color palettes available for inspiration and possible usage. Similar to what we discussed with Adobe Color CC, COLOURlovers.com provides tools for creating colors and palettes from scratch along with free tools for capturing colors from a pixelated image. See References [5, 6] for additional details about the COLOURlovers.com social network. Color Palette Software (COPASO), is the COLOURlovers advanced online color palette tool that allows for creating color schemes from scratch or selecting colors from an uploaded image. Figure 5.8 shows the COPASO user interface.

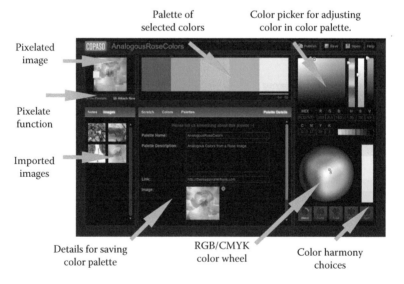

FIGURE 5.8 User interface to the COLOURlovers' Color Palette Software tool (COPASO) that allows for creating a color palette from either applying color harmony choices or from importing a jpeg image. (Image created by Theresa-Marie Rhyne, 2016, with the COPASO online tool at the COLOURlovers' Web site, http://www.colourlovers.com/copaso/ColorPaletteSoftware.)

5.4.1 Creating a Color Palette with COLOURlovers' COPASO

Here we develop a color scheme, with *COPASO*, by choosing a Red hue as a base color, and selecting the Tetrad color harmony option in the lower right hand corner of the tool. As noted in Section 4.5.7, a tetrad harmony encompasses four hues that are equally distant from one another to form a rectangle on the color wheel. Frequently, the result is two complementary pairs of colors. For this example, Red and its opposing or complementary color of Cyan is paired with Yellow and its opposing or complementary color of Blue in RGB color space. COPASO shows these four colors as dots on its RGB/CMYK color wheel located in the bottom right hand corner of the application. By selecting a box in the color palette bar at the top of the COPASO application and then double-clicking on one of the four tetrad colors recommended by the color wheel in the lower right of COPASO, we are able to enter each suggested tetrad hue to form our color scheme at the top of the COPASO application. We named this color palette as *Red based tetrad* and publish it on the COLOURlovers' site as shown in Figure 5.9.

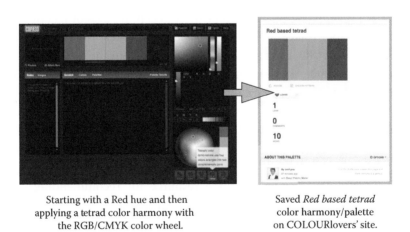

Starting with a Red hue and then applying a tetrad color harmony with the RGB/CMYK color wheel.

Saved *Red based tetrad* color harmony/palette on COLOURlovers' site.

FIGURE 5.9 Building a Tetrad color harmony in the key of Red with the online Color Palette Software (COPASO) tool on the COLOURlovers' Web site. (Image created by Theresa-Marie Rhyne, 2016, using the COPASO online tool at the COLOURlovers' Web site, http://www.colourlovers.com/copaso /ColorPaletteSoftware.)

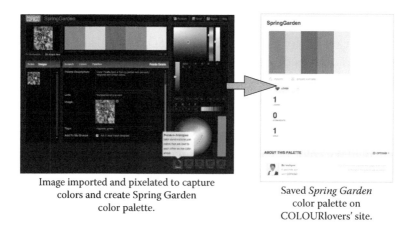

Image imported and pixelated to capture colors and create Spring Garden color palette.

Saved *Spring Garden* color palette on COLOURlovers' site.

FIGURE 5.10   Creating a color palette from an image imported and pixilated to capture colors with the online COPASO (Color Palette Software) tool on the COLOURlovers' Web site. (Image created by Theresa-Marie Rhyne, 2016, using the COPASO online tool at the COLOURlovers' Web site, http://www.colourlovers .com/copaso/ColorPaletteSoftware.)

5.4.2 Capturing a Color Palette from an Image with COLOURlovers' COPASO

The COPASO application can also be used to capture a color palette from an imported jpeg image. In Figure 5.10, we import the *Spring Garden* jpeg image into COPASO and select the *Pixelate* option in the upper left-hand corner of COPASO. After the image is pixelated, we move COPASO's color sensor to select colors for the color palette in the upper center of the application. Once five colors are selected, we name this color palette as *Spring Garden* and publish it on the COLOURlovers site as shown in Figure 5.10.

5.5 COLOR SCHEME DESIGNER: PALETTON.COM

Color Scheme Designer is an online resource for recommending color schemes based on the concepts of artistic (RYB) color theory. While access to the site at www.paletton.com is free, donations are requested to help support the site and keep the resource available online. The application consists of two panels: (1) a color wheel panel for selecting and creating color harmonies on the left and (2) a display panel on the right for assessing how the selected or created color harmony appears. Color Scheme Designer is a robust design tool that includes color harmony suggestions; display views of color schemes, including possible Web pages; color deficiency vision simulations, and tables with Web HEX and RGB values for

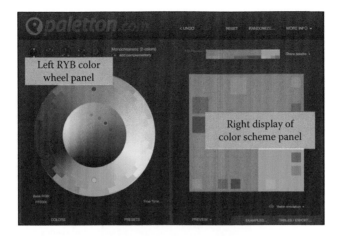

FIGURE 5.11 User interface to the Color Scheme Designer tool (http://www
.paletton.com). (Image created by Theresa-Marie Rhyne, 2016, using the Color
Scheme Designer tool.)

exporting in various formats. We highlight some of the tool's functionality
below. References [7,8] provide additional details about this online tool.
Figure 5.11 shows the user interface for Color Scheme Designer in the key
or base color of Red. This is the default color and hue when Color Scheme
Designer is first accessed.

Central to Color Scheme Designer is a Red, Yellow, and Blue (RYB)
painters color wheel displayed in the left panel of this online tool. The use
of the RYB color wheel differs from many other similar online tools and
apps that use the RGB color wheel. The resulting color harmonies shown
with Color Scheme Designer are in RYB color space and are the *classic*
painter or artistic results. For example, Red is complementary to Green in
the RYB color space. However, in the RGB and CMYK color spaces, Red is
complementary to Cyan. In Chapter 4, we outlined both the RGB/CMYK
and the RYB color wheel and respective color harmonies. For a comparison of RGB/CMYK and RYB color wheel differences, see Figure 4.4.

5.5.1 Left Panel Color Wheel and Color Selection Functions

In addition to the central color wheel, the left panel also includes (1)
color harmony functions in the upper left-hand corner of its color wheel
interface; (2) the ability to set a base or key color with a Web HEX value
in the lower left-hand corner of the color wheel; (3) preset color palettes
that address tints, tones, and shades of a hue as an option in the lower

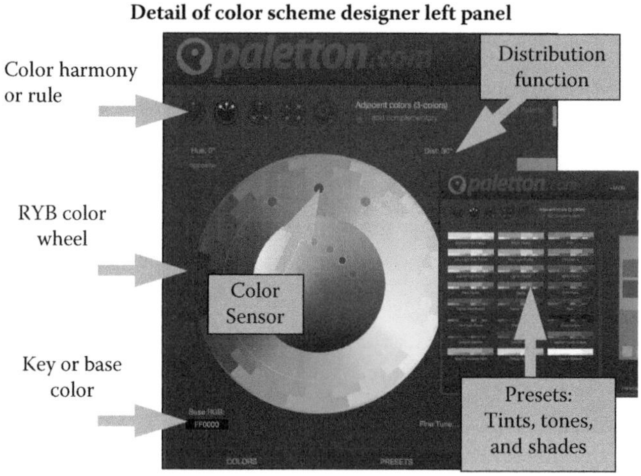

Detail of color scheme designer left panel

Color harmony or rule

Distribution function

RYB color wheel

Color Sensor

Key or base color

Presets: Tints, tones, and shades

FIGURE 5.12   Details of the left panel of the Color Scheme Designer user interface (http://www.paletton.com). (Image created by Theresa-Marie Rhyne, 2016, using the Color Scheme Designer tool.)

right-hand corner of its color wheel interface; (4) the capability to fine-tune colors as an option just above the *Presets* function in the lower right-hand corner of the color wheel; and (5) a distribution function in degrees that allows for setting how close the color sensors on the color wheel should be for color harmony functions with multiple hues such as analogous, triad, and tetrad harmonies. We show these options in Figure 5.12.

5.5.2 Right Panel Display and Vision Simulation Functions

In the right display panel of Color Scheme Designer, the selected color scheme or palette is shown. A general overview of the color scheme is displayed at the top of the right display panel. The central display is controlled by the *Preview* option at the bottom left of the right panel. The *Preview* option allows for viewing the color scheme or palette in various display formats noted as Default, Default with text, Alternative, Alternative with text, Circles, Mondrianish mosaic, Mondrianish mosaic (empty), and others. Earlier in this book, we described a color scheme design based on the Mondrianish mosaic function in Section 1.5. The *Examples* option, the bottom middle button of the right panel, displays a potential Web page design of the selected color scheme. The *Tables /Export* option, the bottom right button of the right panel, displays the Web HEX and RGB values of the selected color scheme as well as allowing for exporting the color values

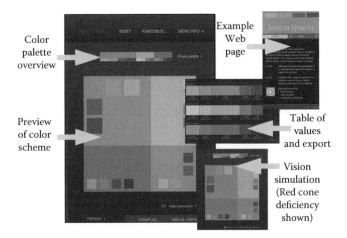

FIGURE 5.13   Details of right panel for the Color Scheme Designer user interface (http://www.paletton.com). (Image created by Theresa-Marie Rhyne, 2016, using the Color Scheme Designer tool.)

as code or color swatches to interface with other content creation tools. These options are shown in Figure 5.13.

The display panel also includes a *vision simulation* icon that allows for selecting a *color blindness* option such as protanomaly (Red cone), deuteranomaly (Green cone), tritanomaly (Blue cone), and other color deficiencies. We covered these and other specific color deficiencies that Color Scheme Designer supports in Section 2.8. A Color Scheme Designer vision simulation for red cone or protanomaly deficiency is shown in Figure 5.13.

5.5.3 Selecting and Implementing a Square-Tetrad Color Scheme

Here, we use Color Scheme Designer to help us select a square-tetrad color scheme of four colors. The work flow process is shown in Figure 5.14. As our first step, we chose the *Alternate* view from the *Preview* function in the right panel of Color Scheme Designer. This allows us to view hues, tints, tones, and shades of the colors we select. Next, we begin working with the RYB color wheel in the left panel to select our key or base color as Orange. To do this, we move the color sensor to the Orange region of the color wheel and notice that we have a monochromatic color scheme. Orange hues, tones, and shades should appear in the right display window. Next we select the Tetrad (four colors) function to find three additional colors with Orange. The complement to Orange, Blue Green on the RYB color wheel is automatically shown to us. The two other colors are light Orange and dark Blue.

We move the dark Blue color sensor into the Purple regions of the color wheel and set a Dist value equal to 90 degrees to create a square (tetrad) color scheme. The complement to Purple is Yellow on Color Scheme Designer's RYB color wheel. As a result we have two complementary pairs of Orange and Blue Green with Purple and Yellow. These colors appear in the right display window panel in Color Scheme Designer as our tetrad (four-color) scheme. To view a vision simulation for Red cone deficiency or protanopia, we select that option from the *Vision Simulation* tab in the lower right-hand corner of the right display panel. The vision simulation indicates that if we stay with the hue values, there will be a sufficient difference between the four colors. The hues of Orange and Yellow will look slightly different to someone with the protanopia color deficiency with Orange appearing to be a darker shade of Yellow. Next, we select the Tables/Export function in the right display panel to view and export the hue values in the Web HEX or RGB format. Figure 5.14 summarizes the steps noted earlier.

Now that we have the Web HEX and RGB values of our four hues, we can use our color scheme for design purposes. For our example, we use

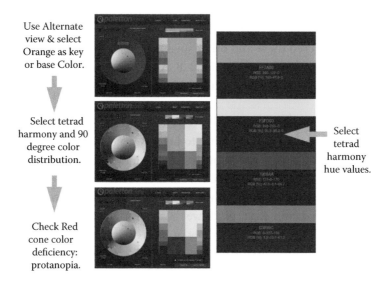

Use Alternate view & select Orange as key or base Color.

Select tetrad harmony and 90 degree color distribution.

Check Red cone color deficiency: protanopia.

Select tetrad harmony hue values.

FIGURE 5.14   Workflow diagram for using the Color Scheme Designer tool (http://www.paletton.com) to create a square-tetrad color scheme in the key or base color of Orange. (Image created by Theresa-Marie Rhyne, 2016, using the Color Scheme Designer tool.)

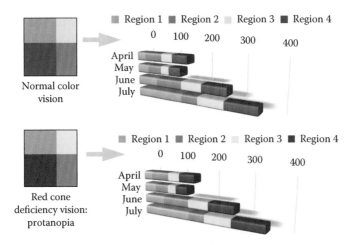

FIGURE 5.15 Applying the square-tetrad color scheme in the key of Orange to the development of a 3D stacked bar infographic with four colors. For this example, we also include the 3D stacked infographic with hues of the Color Scheme Designer's Red cone deficiency (protanopia) vision simulation to help us visualize the protanopia viewer perspective of the infographic. (Image created by Theresa-Marie Rhyne, 2016, using the Color Scheme Designer tool, http://www.paletton.com.)

the sample data set of sales over a 4-month period applied to color harmony examples in Chapter 4 to create an infographic or information visualization. We decide to build a three-dimensional stacked bar chart, created with Apple Numbers and Pages software. To illustrate how our tetrad color scheme for the stacked bar chart might appear to someone with the protanopia Red cone deficiency, we show the protanopia simulation results underneath the normal color vision example. Figure 5.15 summarizes our efforts.

5.6 COLOR COMPANION—ANALYZER AND CONVERTER

Color Companion is a $1.99 app for the iOS iPhone and iPad platforms from Digital Media Interactive LLC. More information about the app is available in iTunes preview at https://itunes.apple.com/us/app/color -companion-analyzer-converter/id477794973?mt=8. The app allows for creating a color palette from (1) an RGB/CMYK color wheel with the help of color harmony guides, (2) an image from an imported Web page, and (3) a camera capture or an imported image from an iPhone or iPad photo library. The app also facilitates mixing two colors to create a third as well as

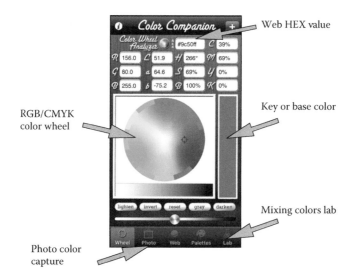

FIGURE 5.16   User interface to the Color Companion app (https://itunes.apple
.com/us/app/color-companion-analyzer-converter/id477794973?mt=8). (Image
created by Theresa-Marie Rhyne, 2016, using the Color Companion app.)

converting color values into Web HEX, RGB, CMYK, Lab, and HSB (hue,
saturation, and brightness) values. We highlighted these various color
value formats in Chapter 3. We also previously featured moving a photo
image into the Color Companion app and examining the color values in
Section 3.9.4. Here, we highlight how to create a color scheme with the
color wheel, provide details of importing a photo image to create a color
palette, and mix two colors to create a third. References [9,10] provide
additional information about features of this mobile app. Figure 5.16 highlights the user interface of the Color Companion app in detail with the key
color of Purple and its respective Web HEX, RGB, Lab, HSB, and CMYK
values are shown.

5.6.1 Creating a Color Scheme with Color Companion's Color Wheel

Here, we use the RGB/CMYK color wheel of Color Companion to begin
the process of creating a color scheme with the provided color harmony
rules. As shown in Figure 5.17, we first select a key or base color from the
color wheel. For our example, the key color is Purple. Next, we tap on
the "+" icon in the upper right of the Color Companion user interface to
move to the *Select Palette* window. From the *Select Palette* window, we
tap on the *Create Color Scheme Palette* to view a set of color harmony

Tap on "+" to obtain
"Select Palette".

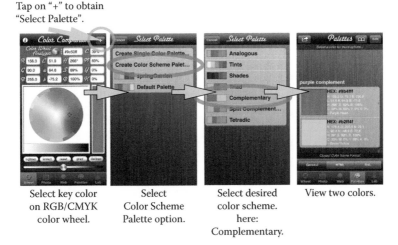

| Select key color on RGB/CMYK color wheel. | Select Color Scheme Palette option. | Select desired color scheme. here: Complementary. | View two colors. |

FIGURE 5.17 Using the Color Companion app for iOS platforms to create a complementary harmony in the key or base color of Purple. (Image created by Theresa-Marie Rhyne, 2016, using the Color Companion app, https://itunes .apple.com/us/app/color-companion-analyzer-converter/id477794973?mt=8.)

options. For this example, we select the *Complementary* option and view the resulting two colors. From Section 4.5.3, we learned that a complementary color harmony combines a key color with the color directly opposing it on the color wheel. For this case, Purple and Yellow Green are complements on the RGB/CMYK color wheel. Our efforts are summarized in Figure 5.17.

5.6.2 Creating a Color Scheme from an Image with Color Companion

Previously, in Section 3.9.4, we showed how to examine the values of a color palette resulting from importing a color image into the Color Companion app. Here, we review the steps of importing our color photo entitled *Spring Garden*. As noted in Figure 5.16, the second icon in the bottom menu bar allows for importing a *Photo* from your iPhone's or iPad's photo library. Touch on this icon to do so and then touch on the resulting *Select Image* button in the upper left hand corner. Once the photo is imported into the Color Companion app, the *Analyze, Analyze and Save*, and *Cancel* options appear at the top of the captured image. Select *Analyze and Save* and Color Companion automatically selects a color from the image as shown in the first image on the left in Figure 5.18. In this example, the key color selected is Magenta.

Auto Analyze function
to generate palette colors.

Two colors selected for
palette.

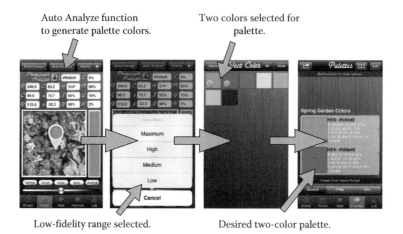

Low-fidelity range selected.

Desired two-color palette.

FIGURE 5.18   Using the Color Companion app for iOS platforms to select two colors from a captured image and create a color scheme. (Image created by Theresa-Marie Rhyne, 2016, using the Color Companion app, https://itunes.apple.com /us/app/color-companion-analyzer-converter/id477794973?mt=8.)

Select *Auto Analyze* to obtain four options of *Maximum*, *High*, *Medium*, *and Low*. For this example, we will select *Low* to receive a display of seven color swatches. Tap on the color swatches that are desired for your color palette. For this example, we will tap on the Magenta color and the Green color. As a result of selecting these two colors, a check box appears beside each color. Select *Done* for Color Companion to build the desired color palette. Next, select on the *Create Multi-Color Palette* option to save the color palette. For this example, we name the palette *Spring Garden Colors* and select the *Create* option. After the color palette is saved, Color Companion returns to the image capture interface. To view the saved color palette, select the *Palettes* icon where the *Spring Garden Colors* are displayed. The two colors of the *Spring Garden Colors* are shown with Web HEX, RGB, Lab, and CMYK values noted. Figure 5.18 summarizes the major steps noted here.

5.6.3 Mixing Colors with Color Companion's Color Lab Function

The Color Companion App provides a *Color Lab* function for creating a blended color from two selected colors. This blending function can aid in determining colors for working in digital media such as photography, visualization, or Web pages as well as assisting in determining potential colors for watercolor or painting studies. To start this process, we select the *Lab* function in the main window of the Color Companion app. The *Lab* icon is the far right icon in the menu bar at the bottom on the main window. We are then transported to the *Color Lab* function where we can enter Web HEX values for the two colors we would like to blend, Color 1 and Color 2. For this example, we select a Green of #4ab54b for Color 1 and a Red of #ff0000 for Color 2. When we select the *light blend* function, we obtain an RGB color blend of Yellow Orange that is specified in Web HEX as #ffb54b. This corresponds to the additive RGB display color model that we highlighted in Section 1.1. The *light blend* value is thus helpful for digital media work. When we select the *paint blend* function, we obtain an RYB color blend of Brownish Yellow that is specified in Web HEX as #9b6d2e. This corresponds to the subtractive RYB painters color model that we highlighted in Section 1.3. The *paint blend* value aids in physical painting work such as watercolor or oil compositions. Figure 5.19 summarizes the Color Companion blending efforts that I have described here.

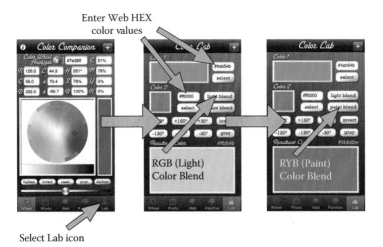

FIGURE 5.19 Using the Color Lab function in the Color Companion app for iOS platforms to blend two colors together to create a new color. (Image created by Theresa-Marie Rhyne, 2016, using the Color Companion app, https://itunes.apple.com/us/app/color-companion-analyzer-converter/id477794973?mt=8.)

5.7 REVISITING THE PANTONE STUDIO FROM SECTION 3.10

As we discussed in Sections 3.10.3 and 3.10.4, the Pantone color-matching system (PMS) is a proprietary color space used primarily in printing and also in a wide range of other industries including cosmetics, colored paint, fabric, and plastics. The PANTONE Studio app is a mobile application that facilitates identifying Pantone values as well as matching colors in a digital image to the Pantone library of colors. The app is a revision to the earlier myPantone app and is currently available on iOS platforms. The Android version is expected to be available in the near future. The basic PANTONE Studio iOS version is free from the iTunes store with a $7.99 monthly subscription providing access to a complete library of Pantone colors. Pantone provides more information about the PANTONE Studio app on their company Web site at https://www. pantone.com/studio. References [11–13] review features of the PANTONE Studio app. Previously in Section 3.10, we showed two main features of the PANTONE Studio app: (1) how to select a Pantone color from a set of digital color swatches in Section 3.10.3 and (2) color capture from a digital image with the PANTONE Studio app in Section 3.10.4. Here, we describe the color *Harmonies* and *Layout* features of the PANTONE Studio app.

5.7.1 Color Harmony with PANTONE Studio PMS Colors

In Section 3.10.3, we showed how to select a Pantone color and its PMS value from the digital color swatches in the PANTONE Studio app. Selecting the Colors menu item and then Your Collection—"Color Bridge" of Pantone colors brings up the digital color swatches. Moving your finger along the color swatches allows for locating a Pantone color. Tapping on a swatch displays the RGB (sRGB), CMYK, and HEX (HTML) values of the selected Pantone color. In Figure 3.24, we showed the selection of a Magenta Pantone color noted as PMS 3527 CP. A selected Pantone color can be dragged into the palette zone, located at the bottom of the app, to store it. Once the Pantone color is in the palette zone, tapping on it reveals a full screen version of the selected color with RGB (sRGB), CMYK, and HEX (HTML) specifications. Sliding your finger upward on the full screen version of the Pantone color reveals Harmonies. The Harmonies option shows monochromatic, analogous, split complementary, triadic, and complementary harmonies based on specified Pantone PMS colors. These concepts were covered in the Section 4.5 discussion on Color Harmony in Chapter 4. Figure 5.20 shows the resulting harmonies for PMS 3527 CP that the PANTONE Studio app specifies.

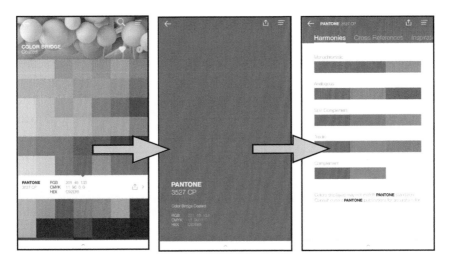

FIGURE 5.20 Color Harmonies specified with the PANTONE Studio app. (Image created by Theresa-Marie Rhyne, 2016, using the the PANTONE Studio app, https://www.pantone.com/studio.)

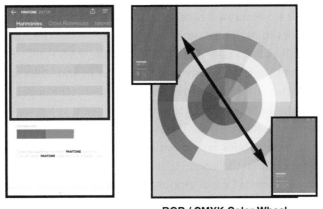

RGB / CMYK Color Wheel

FIGURE 5.21 Complementary color harmony example specified with the PANTONE Studio app. (Image created by Theresa-Marie Rhyne, 2016, using the PANTONE Studio app, https://www.pantone.com/studio.)

The color harmonies specified by the PANTONE Studio app are based on the RGB/CMYK color wheel. To help us visualize these relationships, we depict the PMS 3527 CP (Magenta) color and the 3501 CP (Green) specified complementary color on the RGB/CMYK color wheel that we developed in Chapter 4. These results are shown in Figure 5.21.

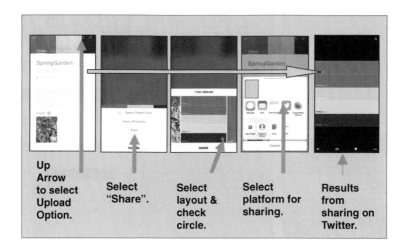

Up Arrow to select Upload Option. Select "Share". Select layout & check circle. Select platform for sharing. Results from sharing on Twitter.

FIGURE 5.22   Sharing the PANTONE Studio color palette and layout via social media. (Image created by Theresa-Marie Rhyne, 2016, using the PANTONE Studio app, https://www.pantone.com/studio.)

5.7.2 Color Texture with PANTONE Studio PMS Colors

In Section 3.10.4, we showed how the PANTONE Studio app can be used to capture colors in an image on a mobile phone. After the image is captured and the Pantone color palette is saved, the PANTONE Studio app provides a layout function for sharing the colors of your selected Pantone palette. To use the *Share* function, tap on the arrow in the upper right hand corner of the desired color palette, in our example it is *Spring Garden*. In the options menus, select *Share*. The Pantone colors of your selected color palette are in various color layout options. Select the layout you desire by tapping on the circle in the lower right hand corner. This results in a check mark appearing. Next a "Share" option appears in the lower bottom of the PANTONE Studio app. It is then possible to share your Pantone color palette on social media sites, via texting, or by email. Figure 5.22 shows the result of our efforts.

5.8 COLORBREWER 2.0: COLOR ADVICE FOR CARTOGRAPHY

ColorBrewer is a freely available online resource for assistance in creating color maps that is available online at http://colorbrewer2.org. It was designed and developed, during 2001 and 2002, by Cynthia A. Brewer and Mark A. Harrower in the GeoVISTA Center at Pennsylvania State University with funding from the U.S. National Science Foundation's Digital Government Program. ColorBrewer 1.0 became available in 2002. A new and rebuilt version of the color tool, entitled *ColorBrewer 2.0*, was developed and donated by Axis Maps LLC in 2009 with the most current version updated in 2013. References [14,15] provide technical details about the development of ColorBrewer. The design of ColorBrewer incorporates aspects of the Munsell Color System. We highlighted the Munsell Color System in Section 3.7.

As indicated by its geographic map like user interface, ColorBrewer was initially designed as *color advice for cartography*, with Cynthia Brewer authoring several books on geographic map design since ColorBrewer's introduction. ColorBrewer 2.0 has gone beyond its original intent with wide usage in the infographics and visualization communities. Many ColorBrewer color schemes are now incorporated into several Geographic Information System (GIS) and data visualization tools with appropriate credit given to the ColorBrewer project. References [16–18] highlight these efforts.

5.8.1 Types of Color Schemes in ColorBrewer 2.0

There are three types of color schemes defined in ColorBrewer: (1) sequential, (2) diverging, and (3) qualitative. Sequential color schemes are aimed at representing data with a logical progression such as from low to high values. The single-hue color palettes provide sequential color schemes that closely approximate monochromatic color harmonies, while the multihue color palettes provide analogous color harmonies. Diverging color schemes are designed for situations where a critical or key break point in the data should be emphasized. For example, in plotting temperature data, the transition from cold to hot temperatures has a mild transition point. Some of the diverging color schemes in ColorBrewer represent complementary color harmonies. Qualitative color schemes use different hues to create a color palette that focuses on the kinds or categories of data, but do not emphasize the order of the data. A geographic map or chart representing the types of agriculture in geographic regions would be an example for the application of a qualitative color scheme. Figure 5.23 shows a detailed view of the three types of color schemes that are specified under the *Nature of your data* menu option in ColorBrewer.

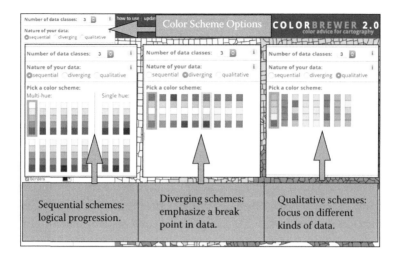

FIGURE 5.23 The three types of color schemes defined in ColorBrewer: (1) sequential, (2) diverging, and (3) qualitative. (Image created by Theresa-Marie Rhyne, 2016, with elements of the ColorBrewer 2.0 tool, http://colorbrewer2.org.)

5.8.2 Using ColorBrewer 2.0 for Selecting a Color Scheme

When ColorBrewer 2.0 is accessed online, the application appears with a set of selection items on the left and a cartographic map with borders drawn on the right. The default setting is the *sequential* and *Multi-hue* Blue Green (noted as BuGn) color scheme. The first step in using ColorBrewer requires determining the *Number of data classes* or the number of variables you want to display with a given chart or map. ColorBrewer starts with three (3) as the lowest number of data classes. The next step with ColorBrewer is to select the *Nature of your data* or the type of color palette desired. We noted these options in the previous discussion in Section 5.8.1 on sequential, diverging, and qualitative color schemes in ColorBrewer. The next step is to select a desired color scheme or palette among the various options provided.

ColorBrewer provides additional options for customizing your color selection process. The *Only Show* items include *colorblind safe*, *print friendly*, and *photocopy safe*. For developing a map, the *Context* items include *roads*, *cities*, and *borders*. The default selection includes *borders* as checked. It is often helpful to unselect the *borders* option so that the cartographic map on the right displays the color scheme without the border boundaries. The *Background* menu allows for selecting *solid color* or *terrain*. The default item is *solid color* and that is the most often used selection from the *Background* menu. The *terrain* function allows for seeing a three-dimensional map terrain underneath the selected color scheme. Once a color scheme is selected, ColorBrewer notes it. For example, the default 3-class Blue Green color scheme is noted as *3-class BuGn* in the menu bar in the lower left corner, adjacent to the cartographic map display. This menu section has icons that note if a color scheme is *colorblind safe, photocopy friendly, laptop or LCD friendly*, and *printer friendly*. The menu button allows for selecting (Web) HEX, RGB, and CMYK color values. The HEX color values are the default option. The *Export* function allows for sharing and exporting the selected color scheme data as (1) a direct Web URL to the selected color scheme, (2) an Adobe color scheme file format for usage with Adobe creative tools, (3) a GIMP color palette, and (4) a cascading style sheet format for further Web development efforts.

We work through an example here to illustrate the usage of ColorBrewer. We desire to select a color scheme for a three-dimensional bar chart for our sample data set of sales over a 4-month period that we used extensively in Chapter 4 and also in earlier Chapter 5 examples. We have data from three regions and in order to depict these, our "Number of data classes" is three (3). Since we do not have an ordered data set or a data set with given break points, we select *qualitative* for the *Nature of your data* option. We select the *colorblind safe* option under the *Only Show* menu and deselect the *borders option* under the *Context* menu. We chose the *3-class Set 2* color scheme or the third and last color scheme counting from the left. Figure 5.24 shows our color scheme selection process.

This chosen color scheme is not considered to be *photocopy friendly*. We accepted this limitation for our infographic design. The specific ColorBrewer 2.0 URL to the qualitative color scheme that we selected is noted at http://colorbrewer2.org/?type=qualitative&scheme=Set2&n=3. This URL shows our color scheme with the borders option selected. Now that we can export the URL or the various HEX, RGB, or CMYK values, we can apply our ColorBrewer 2.0 qualitative color scheme to our three-dimensional bar chart. We show these results in Figure 5.25.

5.8.3 Addressing Photocopy Safe and Printer-Friendly Options

If we want to ensure our ColorBrewer color scheme is *printer friendly* and *photocopy safe*, we select these two options with the *colorblind safe* option

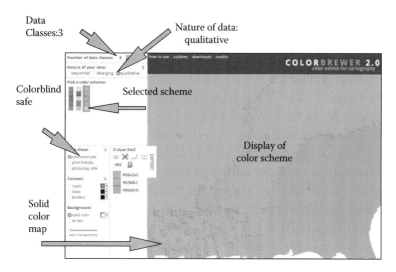

FIGURE 5.24   User interface of ColorBrewer 2.0. (Image created by Theresa-Marie Rhyne, 2016, using ColorBrewer 2.0, http://colorbrewer2.org.)

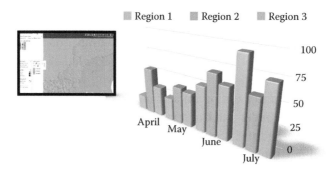

FIGURE 5.25   Applying the *3-class Set2* qualitative color scheme from Color-Brewer 2.0 to a 3D bar chart. (Image created by Theresa-Marie Rhyne, 2016, using ColorBrewer 2.0, http://colorbrewer2.org.)

under the *Only Show* menu. These three options cancel out all of the *qualitative* color schemes under the *Nature of your data* menu. To address this situation, we select the *sequential* option under the *Nature of your data* menu to search for a workable color scheme. Since we do not have data with a break point, we do not select the *diverging* option at this time. We select a Yellow Green Blue (YlGnBu) color palette as a possible option

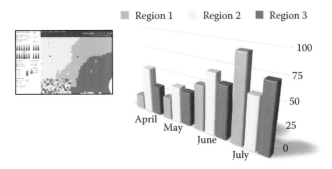

FIGURE 5.26 Applying the Yellow Green Blue (YLGnBU) sequential color scheme from ColorBrewer 2.0 to a 3D bar chart. (Image created by Theresa-Marie Rhyne, 2016, using ColorBrewer 2.0, http://colorbrewer2.org.)

that addresses all three of our *colorblind safe, printer friendly*, and *photocopy safe* criteria. The specific ColorBrewer 2.0 URL to the color scheme that we selected is noted at http://colorbrewer2.org/?type=sequential&scheme=YlGnBu&n=3. Figure 5.26 shows the results of applying the sequential Yellow Green Blue (YlGnBU) color scheme from ColorBrewer 2.0 to our three-dimensional bar chart example to produce the *colorblind safe, printer friendly*, and *photocopy safe* result.

5.8.4 Using ColorBrewer 2.0 with Only Two Variables

An item worth noting here is that if you have only two variables to plot or represent, it is still possible to use ColorBrewer by selecting a diverging color scheme. For a two variable situation, set the *Number of data classes* equal to 3. Next, select the *diverging* button under the *Nature of your data*. The first six palettes under the *diverging* scheme option represent two colors separated by White. If we select only two color hues and eliminate the neutral White color, we have a color scheme for a two variables plot. For our example, we return to our sales data set and plot data for two regions with a three-dimensional stacked area chart. Under diverging color schemes in ColorBrewer 2.0, we select the first option on the left entitled *3-class BrBG* with the specific URL (http://colorbrewer2.org/?type=diverging&scheme=BrBG&n=3). Our color scheme becomes the two colors of Brown and Blue Green that we apply to our three-dimensional stacked area chart. We show these results in Figure 5.27.

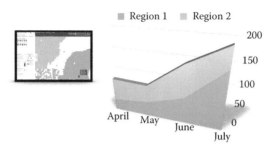

FIGURE 5.27 Applying a three data classes Diverging Color Scheme in ColorBrewer 2.0 to an infographic plot with two colors. (Image created by Theresa-Marie Rhyne, 2016, using ColorBrewer 2.0, http://colorbrewer2.org.)

5.9 REVISITING THE *INTERACTION OF COLOR BY JOSEF ALBERS* APP FROM SECTION 4.8

In Section 4.8, *Modernizing Albers' Interaction of Color Studies with an App*, of Chapter 4 we discussed the mobile iPad app that was developed in 2013 in conjunction with the 50th anniversary editions of the *Interaction of Color* book by Josef Albers. Figure 4.34 illustrated an example of a color study with the iPad app. The app was designed to be a near-digital replica of the 1963 version of *the Interaction of Color* book and is available from the iTunes store for $13.99. The app provides the full version of the text of the book, 125 plates, and over 2 hours of video commentary. Additionally, there are 60 interactive studies where users can create their own color studies with a color wheel palette of over 250 color swatches. When color studies are completed, the color values are saved in Web HEX format and exported as SVG files for use with other software such as the Adobe Photoshop or Illustrator tools. References [19,20] provide information about the book and the app from Yale University Press. Figure 5.28 shows the stages of creating a color study with the *Interaction of Color by Josef Albers* app.

In addition to its function as a teaching app, the *Interaction of Color* app can be used as a design app for creating color palettes and color schemes for future use. Here, we show an example of working with the *Interaction of Color* App and its templates to aid in creating an infographic or information visualization. We begin by working with our completed *color study* in Figure 5.28. We save our color study, export the Web HEX values of each hue in an email, and take a snapshot of our color study work with our iPad camera for safekeeping. We then select five colors from the color study as colors we will use in our future infographic or information visualization.

Next, we work with the sample data set of sales over a 4-month period we used in our color harmony examples in Section 4.5. We build a pie chart of the sales data and then apply the five colors from our color study to the pie chart. Our results are shown in Figure 5.29.

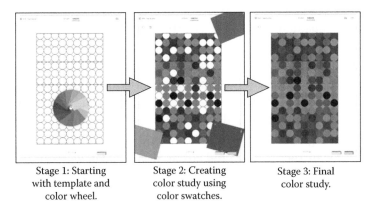

| Stage 1: Starting with template and color wheel. | Stage 2: Creating color study using color swatches. | Stage 3: Final color study. |

FIGURE 5.28 The stages of using the *Interaction of Color by Josef Albers* app to build a color study from one of the provided templates. (Image created by Theresa-Marie Rhyne, 2016, with the *Interaction of Color* App templates, http://yupnet.org/interactionofcolor/. The templates are copyrighted by Yale University Press. With permission from Yale University Press.)

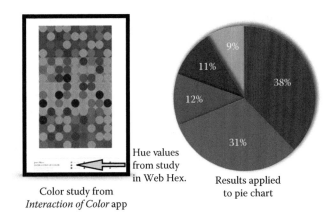

Color study from
Interaction of Color app

Hue values from study in Web Hex.

Results applied to pie chart

FIGURE 5.29 Applying a color study created with the *Interaction of Color by Josef Albers* iPad App to an infographic (pie chart). (Image created by Theresa-Marie Rhyne, 2016, with the *Interaction of Color* App templates, http://yupnet.org/interactionofcolor/. The templates are copyrighted by Yale University Press. With permission from Yale University Press.)

5.10 CONCLUDING REMARKS

In Chapter 5, we have examined eight tools for analyzing and creating color palettes. These include the following: (1) Adobe Color CC, (2) Adobe Capture CC, (3) the COLOURlovers community and its Color Palette Software (COPASO) tool, (4) Paletton's Color Scheme Designer, (5) Color Companion, (6) PANTONE Studio, (7) ColorBrewer 2.0, and (8) *Interaction of Color by Josef Albers* iPad app. We discussed key features of each tool and showed how each respective tool can be used to analyze or create a color palette. Each tool has its own particular approach for aiding in creating and assessing color schemes. As you continue on in your color studies, you will likely find additional color applications that work as part of your own digital color toolbox. At the end of this chapter, we provide references for further reading and online access to details about the color tools that we have discussed in this chapter. In the next chapter, Chapter 6, we will discuss how some of these tools were used to address specific color palette requirements for selected case study examples.

REFERENCES

1. Adobe Systems Incorporated. (2016). Adobe Color. Available at https://color.adobe.com
2. Designer's Lab. (2014). How to Work with Adobe Color CC (Adobe Kuler) to Enhance your Designs. Available at http://www.sweet-web-design.com/wordpress/how-to-work-with-adobe-color-cc-adobe-kuler-to-enhance-your-designs/2320/
3. Adobe Systems Incorporated. (2016). Adobe Capture CC. Available at http://www.adobe.com/products/capture.html
4. Adobe Systems Incorporated. (2016). Introducing Adobe Capture CC, Moving Colors: The Adobe SpeedGrade Blog. Available at http://blogs.adobe.com/movingcolors/2015/10/05/introducing-adobe-capture-cc/
5. Monsef, I.V. and Darius A. (2011). *Color Inspirations: More than 3,000 Innovative Palettes from the Colourlovers.com Community.* Cincinnati, OH: HOW Books.
6. Creative Market Labs, Inc. (2016). COLOURlovers.com. Available at http://www.colourlovers.com/
7. Stanicek, P. and ColorSchemeDesigner.com. (2011). Usage, ColorScheme-Designer Blog. Available at http://www.colorschemedesigner.com/blog/usage/
8. Paletton.com. (2016). Color Scheme Designer. Available at http://paletton.com.
9. Digital Media Interactive LLC. (2012). Color Companion—Analyzer & Converter. Available at https://itunes.apple.com/us/app/color-companion-analyzer-converter/id477794973?mt=8

10. iPad Daily App. (2012). Color Companion: Choose the Perfect Color for You. Available at http://365app4u.blogspot.com/2012/03/color-companion-choose-perfect-color.html

11. Co.Design. (2016). Pantone's Addictive New App Turns The World Into A Prismatic Palette. Available at http://www.fastcodesign.com/3062394/pantones-addictive-new-app-turns-the-world-into-a-prismatic-palette

12. Pantone. (2016). Studio. Available at https://www.pantone.com/studio

13. Dexigner. (2016), PANTONE Studio: New App Brings Insta-Ready Color & Inspiration to Your Device, Available at: http://www.dexigner.com/news/29182.

14. Brewer, C.A., Hatchard, G.W., and Harrower, M.A. (2003). ColorBrewer in Print: A catalog of color schemes for maps. *Cartography and Geographic Information Science*, 30(1): 5–32.

15. Harrower, M.A. and Brewer, C.A. (2003). ColorBrewer.org. An online tool for selecting color schemes for maps. *The Cartographic Journal*, 40(1): 27–37.

16. Brewer, C.A. (2015). *Designing Better Maps: A Guide for GIS Users*, Second Edition. Redlands, CA: ESRI Press.

17. Brewer, C.A. and Harrower, M. (2016). ColorBrewer 2.0: Color Advice for Cartography. Available at http://colorbrewer2.org

18. Krzywinski, M. (2016). Brewer Palettes. Available at http://mkweb.bcgsc.ca/brewer/

19. Albers, J. (2013). *Interaction of Color*, 50th Anniversary Edition. New Haven, CT: Yale University Press.

20. Yale University Press. (2016). Interaction of Color App for iPad. Available at http://yupnet.org/interactionofcolor/

CHAPTER 6

Case Study Examples of Colorizing Visualizations

I N THIS CHAPTER, we present three examples of projects that applied principles of color theory to data visualization. These examples use color theory to provide insight into the particular problem under study. The three case studies include (1) identification of patterns associated with correlation in biological data, (2) examining the level of household broadband availability in geographic communities, and (3) exploring the impacts of climate change in regard to the development of tropical storms.

6.1 COLOR STUDY: VISUALIZING BIOLOGICAL DATA

The process of detecting novel patterns of correlation in large-scale molecular biological data can aid in discovering the existence of previously unknown cellular regulatory mechanisms. Researchers have successfully applied the mathematical modeling of DNA microarray data to correctly predict previously unknown global modes of regulation for genes. For further reading on such efforts, see [1]. In a project with the Scientific Computing and Imaging (SCI) Institute at the University of Utah, we applied color theory principles to aid in creating a visualization approach to support this type of research. Central to our biological visualization efforts was the recognition that our research scientists would be working in a Red, Green, and Blue (RGB) color display environment and could have color vision deficiencies. A key objective was to design a color scheme that would aid in detecting patterns for correlation in the large-scale molecular biological data. The visible light spectrum and other color vision principles were discussed in Chapter 2.

6.1.1 Using the Munsell Color Order System for Biological Data Visualization Inspiration

Our first contribution involved exploring visual design approaches for creating the display of a global view that depicts the temporal aspects of protein activity. The local views of protein activity incorporated concise representations of statistical measures. A tiled view that combined several local views of data was proposed for the global view. We found inspiration from two-dimensional cross sections of the Munsell color order system, in developing the tiled view concept. In Section 3.7.2.3 Chroma, we described how chroma values are depicted in the Munsell color order system, with Figure 3.13 depicting differences in chroma scales for a Red (5R) hue and its complement Blue Green (5BG) hue. For our visualization of a global view of protein activity, we explored combining the merger of the (10GY) Munsell Green Yellow hue with the complement (10P) Munsell Purple hue as a mock-up display concept. Figure 6.1 shows the merger of the Munsell 10 GY and the Munsell 10 P cross sections on the left and how this layout aided building the global view of temporal relationships between biological variables on the right. Reference [2] highlights our approach in further detail. We used the digital Munsell hue, value, and chroma and International Commission on Illumination (CIE) x, y, and Y data from the Munsell Color Science Laboratory at Rochester Institute of Technology (http://www.cis.rit.edu/research/mcsl2/online/) for the Munsell color cross sections on the left-hand side in Figure 6.1.

6.1.2 Selecting the Color Scheme for the Biological Data Visualization

In our visualization efforts, we desired to have a global tile view that also incorporated the local views' concise representations of statistical measures. To complete our biological data visualization, we required a color scheme of two contrasting hues. When global views of the biological data were calculated for visualization, a series of tints for each color evolved to correspond to localized data variances in the global tiled view. As we discussed in Section 4.3.2 of Chapter 4, a tint is a hue mixed with White. Tints vary from small to large percentages of White mixed with the original hue. Our biological visualization would include a range of tints for the two contrasting hues of the color scheme. Although we initially

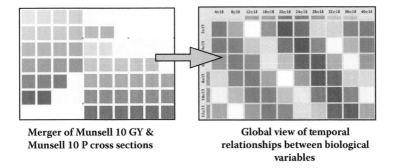

| Merger of Munsell 10 GY & Munsell 10 P cross sections | Global view of temporal relationships between biological variables |

FIGURE 6.1   Using Munsell color cross sections as a mock-up for a global view of temporal relationships in biological variables. (Illustration created by Theresa-Marie Rhyne, 2011 and 2013, in consulting work with the Scientific Computing and Imaging [SCI] Institute at the University of Utah and posted in the Color Blog by Munsell Color in 2013. See Rhyne, T.-M., Biological Data Visualization Using the Munsell Color System, Color Blog of Munsell Color, 2013.)

proposed combining the Munsell 10 Green Yellow and Munsell 10 Purple colors as potential contrasting hues, we desired to examine further possible options available to us. Since members of the research team had color deficiencies, we also incorporated the notion of addressing color blindness criteria in building the desired color scheme.

We began our consideration of color schemes with two traditional color schemes used in biological data display (1) a Red and Green color map with fully saturated (pure) hues and (2) a Blue and Yellow color map with fully saturated (pure) hues. Figure 6.2 shows the implementation of these two color schemes with the local views' representations of statistical measures incorporated into the global tile views. The variance in tints of the hues corresponding to each color scheme is shown in the visualizations of the biological data.

In order to address color deficiency issues, we ran color deficiency tests with the Vischeck color blindness simulation tool for the Red–Green and Blue–Yellow color palettes [3]. The simulations included (1) the deuteranopia (Green cone) color deficiency, (2) the protanopia (Red cone) color deficiency, and (3) the tritanopia (Blue cone) deficiency. We described each of these color deficiencies previously in Section 2.8. Our desire was to develop a color scheme for the biological visualization that would be discernable for all of these three main types of color deficiencies. As anticipated, the color deficiency simulations showed the proposed color palettes were challenging for individuals with color deficiencies. Figure 6.3

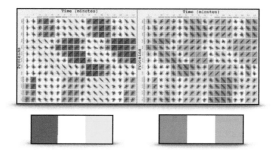

FIGURE 6.2 Traditional Blue–Yellow and Red–Green color palettes applied to examining global correlation of large-scale molecular biological data. (Illustration created by Theresa-Marie Rhyne, 2011, in consulting work with the Scientific Computing and Imaging (SCI) Institute at the University of Utah. See Choudhury, A.N.M.I. et al., Visualizing Global Correlation in Large-Scale Molecular Biological Data, Biovis 2011 Abstracts, Proceedings of the First IEEE Symposium on Biological Data Visualization, Providence, RI, 2011.)

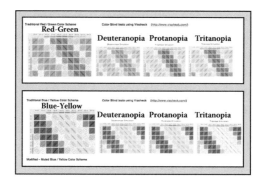

FIGURE 6.3 Color deficiency simulations with Vischeck of Red–Green and Blue–Yellow color schemes. (Illustration created by Theresa-Marie Rhyne, 2011, in consulting work with the Scientific Computing and Imaging [SCI] Institute at the University of Utah.)

summarizes the results from the Vischeck color blindness simulations for the Red–Green and Blue–Yellow color palettes.

As a next step in selecting color schemes, we decided to include Blue–Red and Green–Purple color palette options. While the Blue–Red color palette is not a complementary color harmony, the color combination tests well in regard to providing sufficient color contrast in color deficiency simulations. Our hope was that the Green–Purple palette might test similar to the Blue–Red palette for color deficiency viewers while also being a complementary color harmony for normal color vision viewers.

In Section 4.5.3 of Chapter 4, we covered the concept of complementary color harmony. Figure 6.4 summarizes the results from the Vischeck color blindness simulations for the Red–Blue and Green–Purple color palettes.

Fortunately, the Green–Purple color palette tested positively in providing sufficient color contrast in color deficiency simulations while also satisfying the condition of being a complementary color harmony for individuals with normal color vision. As a result, we selected the Green–Purple color palette as our color scheme for the visualization of global correlation in the large-scale molecular biological data effort. Using Adobe Kuler, now called Adobe Color CC [4], we specified Green and Purple hues according to a complementary color harmony. In a complementary color harmony, the two hues directly oppose each other on the color wheel. In the actual execution of the computational results associated with the large-scale molecular biological data, there are variances between the designed and the finalized Green and Purple hues. Reference [5] discusses additional details of our final results. Figure 6.5 depicts the implementation of our Green–Purple color scheme with the biological data as well as the illustration of the complementary color harmony using Adobe Color CC.

6.1.3 Summary of Results for Colorizing Biological Data Case Study

In this case study, we have discussed how color theory concepts were applied to the visualization of correlation in large-scale molecular biological data. We showed how the merger of the (10GY) Munsell Green–Yellow hue with the complement (10P) Munsell Purple hue in the Munsell

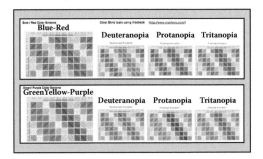

FIGURE 6.4 Color deficiency simulations with Vischeck of Blue–Red and Green–Purple color schemes. (Illustration created by Theresa-Marie Rhyne, 2011, in consulting work with the Scientific Computing and Imaging [SCI] Institute at the University of Utah.)

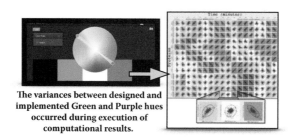

The variances between designed and implemented Green and Purple hues occurred during execution of computational results.

FIGURE 6.5 Selected Green–Purple color scheme applied to examining global correlation of large-scale molecular biological data. (From Choudhury, A.N.M.I. et al., Visualizing Global Correlation in Large-Scale Molecular Biological Data, Biovis 2011 Abstracts, Proceedings of the First IEEE Symposium on Biological Data Visualization, Providence, RI, 2011. Composite illustration created by Theresa-Marie Rhyne, 2011, in consulting work with the Scientific Computing and Imaging [SCI] Institute at the University of Utah and modified in 2016 to depict the Adobe Color CC analysis.)

color order system served as a mock-up display for building a global view concept. We then addressed that our research scientists could have color vision deficiencies while working with our visualization in an RGB color display environment. We addressed these color deficiency issues by testing various color schemes with the Vischeck color blindness simulator. Our final Green–Purple color scheme was selected since the color palette tested positively in providing sufficient color contrast in color deficiency simulations while also satisfying the condition of being a complementary color harmony for individuals with normal color vision. Interestingly, the selected Green–Purple color scheme has strong similarities to the merger of the (10GY) Munsell Green Yellow hue with the complement (10P) Munsell Purple hue that we began with in exploring the global view layout. For more information on the types of research conducted in the Scientific Computing and Imaging Institute (SCI) at the University of Utah [6], see their Web site at http://sci.utah.edu/. Figure 6.6 visually summarizes the key points of this colorizing biological data case study.

6.2 COLOR STUDY: HOUSEHOLD BROADBAND AVAILABILITY

The ability to have broadband access, first responder communications, and classroom connectivity across a given region has become critical to daily operations in a community. Many states in the United States have set up broadband infrastructure offices as statewide efforts to expand

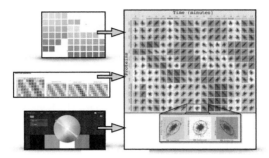

FIGURE 6.6   Visual summary for colorizing biological data case study. Composite illustration created by Theresa-Marie Rhyne, 2016.)

high-speed Internet access, especially to rural or underdeveloped regions. The state of North Carolina currently has a Broadband Infrastructure Office (BroadbandIO) established in 2015 [7]. Prior to 2015, the state of North Carolina had an e-NC authority office that advocated for increased broadband adoption in rural counties and distressed urban areas in North Carolina. The e-NC authority initiative sunset in 2011. In this case study, we discuss an approach to colorizing broadband access data for the 100 counties in the state of North Carolina for the 2002 year. These historic data were available from the e-NC authority. The most current data on the state of North Carolina's broadband infrastructure are openly available from the NC BroadbandIO office at https://ncbroadband.gov/map-resources/. The initial concepts for this case study evolved from prior work with North Carolina State University and the Renaissance Computing Institute at the University of North Carolina at Chapel Hill. References [7,8] provide additional details on household broadband efforts across the state of North Carolina.

6.2.1 Selecting the Color Scheme to Depict Broadband Availability

Using the broadband access data for 2002, we grouped the household availability data according to each of the 100 counties in the state of North Carolina. Next, we determined it would be optimal to use a different color at each 20% threshold level for household broadband availability ranging from 0% to 100%. We also desired our color scheme to emphasize the mid-range value of 70% broadband availability for a given county. We also decided to make a three-dimensional map where the height of each county would also correspond to the level of household broadband availability. A county with 10% broadband availability would have a lower height than a county with 80% broadband availability. To emphasize the three-dimensional quality of the map, the color and height values would dominate visually with the county borders being slightly detectable.

Using the criteria noted above, we used ColorBrewer 2.0 (http://colorbrewer2.org) to help select a color scheme for the broadband access map [9]. We described the process for selecting a color palette using ColorBrewer 2.0 in Section 5.8.2. The number of data classes for our data corresponded to 5, since we had five 20% threshold levels across household broadband availability ranging from 0% to 100%. The nature of our data was *diverging*, since our intent was to emphasize a mid-range value of 70% with extreme values of no broadband availability at 0% and complete broadband availability at 100%. Since we expected there would be both printed and photocopy versions made of our broadband access map, we also selected the *Only Show* features in ColorBrewer 2.0 to be *print friendly* and *photocopy safe*. We did not select the *colorblind safe* option since this would have eliminated all of the *diverging* color schemes. We also deselected the *borders* option under the *Context* features since we did not intend to emphasize the county borders in our three-dimensional map. We kept the default setting of *solid color* for the *Background* features and changed the *background* color to be Black (#000). The result of our ColorBrewer 2.0 selections is shown as the top image in Figure 6.7. Only one color scheme satisfied these criteria and we implemented it in our map of *Household Broadband Availability in the State of North Carolina for the Year of 2002*. This implementation is shown as the bottom image in Figure 6.7. The ColorBrewer 2.0 URL to our selected

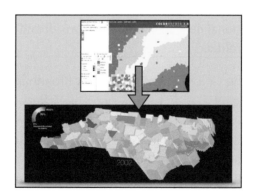

FIGURE 6.7 Using ColorBrewer 2.0 to build a color scheme for a map. (Illustration created by Theresa-Marie Rhyne, 2010 and 2016, using ColorBrewer 2.0, http://colorbrewer2.org.)

color scheme with borders noted and a background color of White is http://
colorbrewer2.org/?type=diverging&scheme=Spectral&n=5.

6.2.2 Determining Cyan, Magenta, Yellow, and Key Black (CMYK) and Pantone Hues for Printing the Map

Although ColorBrewer 2.0 provides us with the CMYK color specifications for printing the ColorBrewer color scheme we selected for our map, we
decided to use the PANTONE Studio app with a digital version of our actual
household broadband map to specify printer colors [10]. These Pantone
color specifications will allow us to work with printing professionals to create a high-quality color reproduction of our map. We described the process
of using the PANTONE Studio app to color capture from a digital image in
Section 3.10.4.

The first step in using the PANTONE Studio app involved importing
a snapshot photo or jpeg image of our *Household Broadband Availability
in the State of North Carolina for the Year of 2002* into the PANTONE
Studio app. After the image was imported, we brushed over the digital
image to select myPantone hues to specify for high-end color printing.
The PANTONE Studio app allowed us to specify a palette of five colors in
a given working session. We specified the Red Orange hue as PMS 2429
CP, the light Yellow hue as PMS 7403 U, the Green hue as PMS 2455CP,
the light Blue hue as PMS 0821 U, and the Dark Blue hue as PMS 3538 U.
We placed the corresponding Pantone hues in the lower menu dock of the
PANTONE Studio app. We thus obtained the five Pantone hues that we
wanted to specify for the high-end color printing of our household broadband availability map. Figure 6.8 visually summarizes our PANTONE

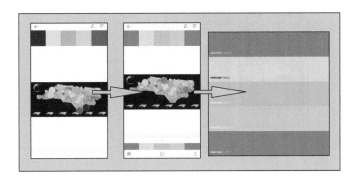

FIGURE 6.8   Using the PANTONE Studio app to capture Pantone hues for potential high-end color printing. (Illustration created by Theresa-Marie Rhyne, 2010
and 2016, using the PANTONE Studio app, https://www.pantone.com/studio.)

Studio color capture efforts for the *Household Broadband Availability in the State of North Carolina for the year of 2002 map.*

6.2.3 Using the Adobe Capture CC for Color Harmony Evaluation

We used the Adobe Capture CC app (http://www.adobe.com/products /capture.html) to analyze the color harmony associated with our household broadband availability map [11]. As noted in our prior discussion of the app in Chapter 5, the Adobe Capture CC app is a free tool for Android and iOS platforms that allows for capturing colors from photos on your mobile device. For more details on the Adobe Capture CC app: see Section 5.3. Using a snapshot photo of our household broadband availability map and the five color sensors in the Adobe Capture CC app, we select the Blue, Green, Yellow, Orange, and Red Orange colors from the map image to create our color scheme. We save the color scheme as *Household Broadband Colors.* The results of our color capture efforts are shown as the left image in Figure 6.9.

For our purposes, we want to use the RGB/CMYK color wheel in Adobe Capture CC to determine the color harmony of the *Household Broadband Availability in the State of North Carolina for the Year of 2002* map. From the color wheel of the app, shown as the middle image in Figure 6.9, we determine that the Red Orange, Orange, Yellow, and Yellow Green colors are adjacent to each other and form an analogous harmony. The Blue hue creates an opposing or complementary color to the previous analogous four colors. This results in an analogous complementary harmony on the color wheel. We highlighted the analogous complementary harmony in Section 4.5.5. The final color scheme with the household broadband

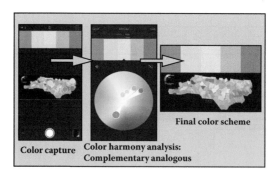

FIGURE 6.9   Using the Adobe Capture CC app to evaluate the color harmony in the *Household Broadband Availability in the State of North Carolina for the Year of 2002* map. (Image created by Theresa-Marie Rhyne, 2016, using the Adobe Capture CC app, http://www.adobe.com/products/capture.html.)

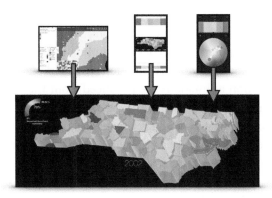

FIGURE 6.10   Visual summary for colorizing household broadband availability case study. (Illustration created by Theresa-Marie Rhyne, 2016.)

availability map is shown as the right image in Figure 6.9. The Adobe Capture CC app is an effective tool for quickly establishing color schemes and resulting color harmonies from snapshot images.

6.2.4 Summary of Results for Colorizing Broadband Availability Case Study

The final map of *Household Broadband Availability in the State of North Carolina for the Year of 2002* included a color scheme ranging from Red Orange as the lowest value, progressing through Orange, Yellow, Green, and Light Blue for middle values and ending in Dark Blue as the highest value. This implementation inverted the ColorBrewer 2.0 suggested scheme that we noted at http://colorbrewer2.org/?type=diverging &scheme=Spectral&n=5. For our efforts, this was an effective color solution for emphasizing counties with little or no household broadband. We used the PANTONE Studio app to specify Pantone colors for working with printing professionals to create a high-quality color reproduction of our map. The Adobe Capture CC app was also used to help us identify the complementary analogous harmony associated with our household broadband map. Figure 6.10 visually summarizes the key points of this colorizing household broadband availability case study.

6.3 COLOR STUDY: TROPICAL STORM ANIMATION

The impact of climate change on the severity of tropical storms is a grand challenge research topic of interest at the national and international levels. Weather scientists have and continue to explore the impacts of warmer water temperatures, higher carbon dioxide levels in the atmosphere, and higher coastal water levels on future hurricane seasons. This type of research requires the use of supercomputers to run detailed simulations of real and theoretical tropical storm models. For further reading on such efforts, see Reference [12]. High-resolution animations are produced from the resulting massive data sets to obtain increased understanding of the structural evolution of the tropical storms. Colorization of data elements helps in tracking the path of a particular parcel of air as well as in observing the different parameters associated with the tropical storm. Here, we present a case study on building a color scheme for the time series animation sequence of a tropical storm or hurricane. A short movie was developed for presentation of final scientific results to the United States Department of Energy (DOE), who funded these research efforts. Reference [13] highlights specific aspects of the movie project. The concepts presented here evolved in prior work with atmospheric and computational scientists at North Carolina State University and the Renaissance Computing Institute at the University of North Carolina at Chapel Hill.

6.3.1 Building a Color Scheme for the Hurricane Animation Sequence

In developing time series animation sequences from the computational tropical storm data, we needed to design color maps that combined data associated with (1) the rain water mixing ratio, (2) the long wave–infrared–radiation reaching the ground surface (*GLW*), and (3) the wind velocity. We also required a land mask in the animation sequence to provide geographic reference for the data set. For our visualization, the rain water mixing ratio data would be used to create isosurfaces. An isosurface represents points of constant value (e.g., pressure or temperature) within a volume of space. Additionally, the *GLW* data values increase with the presence of clouds, especially low clouds that might be associated with rainfall.

We decided to use ColorBrewer 2.0 to develop a proposed color scheme for the stages in the time series animation where the storm was most intense. Under these circumstances, the rain water mixing ratio and *GLW* variables would be tightly coupled and the circling wind vectors superimposed over the resulting isosurfaces. To ensure an effective contrast between the isosurfaces and the wind vectors, we defined the nature of our data to be *diverging* and selected four data classes in ColorBrewer 2.0. We also checked the *colorblind safe*, *print friendly*, and *photocopy safe* options in the *Only Show* menu to address the widest audience of viewers as well as the potential for producing paper copies of the tropical storm imagery. Additionally, the *borders* option was deselected under the *Context* menu so we could easily view how the colors might interact together. After all these options were selected, the Purple and Orange four-classes color scheme remained in ColorBrewer2.0. We selected Purple as the color for the isosurfaces and Orange as the color of the wind vectors. Figure 6.11 shows the selection of the Purple and Orange color scheme in ColorBrewer 2.0 and the implementation of the color scheme on a still frame of the tropical storm animation using the VisIt visualization tool. The Purple Orange color scheme from ColorBrewer can also be viewed, with the borders noted, at the following URL: http:// colorbrewer2.org/?type=diverging&scheme=PuOr&n=4. We will highlight the VisIt tool further in Section 6.3.2 of this color study.

6.3.2 Designing Color Maps for the Visualization/Animation Software

VisIt, an open source data visualization and animation tool, was used to create the tropical storm isosurfaces and time series animation in this color study. VisIt was originally developed by the U.S. DOE's Advanced Simulation and Computing Initiative (ASCI) to visualize and analyze results from extremely large (terascale) simulations. More information about VisIt can be found at https://wci.llnl.gov/simulation/computer -codes/visit/ [14]. Visualization and data scientists imported data sets from the tropical storm simulations into VisIt to produce the resulting isosurfaces and time series animations. Each data set required its own unique color map. We could quickly established dark Orange as the hue for the color map of the wind velocity data set from our prior ColorBrewer work. The rain water mixing ratio data set and the *GLW* data set each required their own color maps, respectively. For these two color maps in

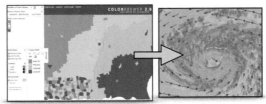

Proposed color scheme for
the Tropical storm animation.

Color Scheme implemented
on a still frame from the
Tropical storm animation.

FIGURE 6.11   Using ColorBrewer 2.0 to propose a color scheme for a tropical storm animation. Illustration created by Theresa-Marie Rhyne, 2009 and 2016, using ColorBrewer 2.0 [http://colorbrewer2.org] and VisIt [https://wci.llnl.gov /simulation/computer-codes/visit/].)

VisIt, we chose a Magenta color for the rain water mixing ratio data set. As noted previously, *GLW* data values increase with the presence of clouds, especially low clouds that might be associated with rainfall. We designed a graduated color map moving from Blue to White for the *GLW* data. We anticipated that White values would appear around the regions of the rain water isosurfaces. To complete our color selection process, for the land mask, we used a map with a dark Blue hue for the land and a Blue Green hue for the ocean regions. If there were lower values of the *GLW* data, we wanted to assure their appearance against the land mask.

On a display monitor, pixels are used to generate the color and representations for this visualization. If two distinct colors each representing different elements of the visualization are in very close proximity, a color illusion is easily created. We highlighted these concepts in Section 4.7.5 in our discussions on Michel Chevreul's principles of color harmony and color contrasts. For our tropical storm visualization, we desired to create an analogous color harmony that potentially blended the Magenta rain water mixing ratio data with the Blue Green mask for the oceans and the Dark Blue mask for the land masses. This would create the Purple hues for our desired Purple Orange color scheme.

At the time of our visualization efforts, we did not have the Color Companion app available to us. However, today, this app could be used to assist in this type of color map selection process [15]. As noted in Section 5.6.3, the Color Companion app provides a *Color Lab* function for creating a blended color from two selected colors. We could reverse engineer the blending function to find two hues that would produce the desired blended Purple. Figure 6.12 shows the use of the Color Companion app to yield the Magenta and Blue Green hues for our respective rain water mixing ratio and Blue Green ocean/land mask in VisIt.

6.3.3 Using Color Scheme Designer for Color Harmony Assessment

Using Paletton's online Color Scheme Designer tool (www.paletton.com; [16]), we can examine the color harmonies of our tropical storm visualization. We covered the Color Scheme Designer tool in Section 5.5. The Blue, Purple, and Magenta hues that created the display of the rain water isosurfaces and *GLW* cloud cover form an analogous color harmony. The Orange and Blue Green hues that depicted the wind vectors against the ocean–land mass mask form a complementary color scheme. Figure 6.13 shows these two color harmonies with the tropical storm visualization.

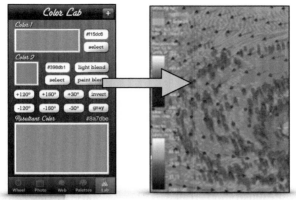

Selecting Magenta & Blue Green colors to yield a Purple blend for rain water isosurfaces.

Applying Magenta colormap against Blue Green ocean/land mask.

FIGURE 6.12 Using the Color Companion app to locate two hues that will blend to create Purple for the Purple Orange color scheme of the tropical storm animation. (Illustration created by Theresa-Marie Rhyne, 2009 and 2016, using the Color Companion app [https://itunes.apple.com/us/app/color-companion-analyzer-converter/id477794973?mt=8] and VisIt [https://wci.llnl.gov/simulation/computer-codes/visit/].)

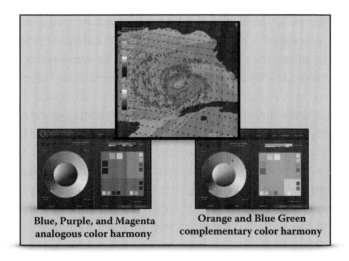

Blue, Purple, and Magenta analogous color harmony

Orange and Blue Green complementary color harmony

FIGURE 6.13 Using Paletton's Color Scheme Designer to depict the color schemes of the tropical storm visualization. Composite illustration created by Theresa-Marie Rhyne, 2009 and 2016, using Paletton's Color Scheme Designer tool [www.paletton.com] and VisIt [https://wci.llnl.gov/simulation/computer-codes/visit/].)

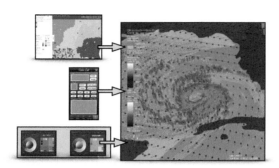

FIGURE 6.14 Visual summary for colorizing a tropical storm animation case study. Composite illustration created by Theresa-Marie Rhyne, 2016.)

6.3.4 Summary of Results for Colorizing a Tropical Storm Animation

The tropical storm animation sequence discussed here combined a Blue, Purple, and Magenta analogous color scheme with an Orange and Blue Green complementary color scheme to amplify the resulting Purple rain water isosurfaces and Orange wind vectors [17]. In the color study, we used ColorBrewer to help define a Purple and Orange color scheme for the completed animation. We then showed how the Color Lab function of the Color Companion app could be used to specify individual colormaps for data variables in the VisIt visualization and animation software. When the data variables are combined to produce the animation sequence, Purple isosurfaces associated with the evolution of the hurricane and Orange wind vectors noting the wind direction during the storm result. The animated time series sequence is used in tracking the path and observing the different parameters of the computationally generated tropical storm. The application of color theory principles and the colorization of data variables aid in amplifying the final visual results. We used Paletton's online Color Scheme Designer tool to depict the Blue, Purple, and Magenta analogous color harmony of the rain water isosurfaces and *GLW* cloud cover as well as the Orange and Blue Green complementary color harmony of the wind vectors against the ocean–land mass mask. Figure 6.14 visually summarizes the key points of this colorizing a tropical storm animation case study.

6.4 CONCLUDING REMARKS

In this chapter, we highlighted three projects that applied principles of color theory to data visualization. The first project discussed how color theory concepts were applied to the visualization of correlation in large-scale molecular biological data. The second project described the development of a household broadband availability map for the state of North Carolina. The third project applied principles of color harmony and color contrasts to depicting the times series animation for a computationally modeled tropical storm. The previous sections and chapters in this book that described the various color theory principles and color analysis tools discussed in Chapter 6 were noted in each case study discussion. At the end of this chapter, we provide references for further reading or online access to material we have discussed in these case studies. In Chapter 7, we review the basic color theory concepts and color analysis tools covered throughout this book.

REFERENCES

1. Alter, O. and Golub, G.H. (2004). Integrative analysis of genome-scale data by using pseudoinverse projection predicts novel correlation between DNA replication and RNA transcription. *Proceedings of the National Academy of Sciences of the United States of America*, 1001: 16577–16582.
2. Rhyne, T.-M. (2013). Biological Data Visualization Using the Munsell Color System, Color Blog of Munsell Color. Available at http://munsell.com /color-blog/biological-data-visualization-tools/, accessed June 13, 2016.
3. Vischeck. (2016). About Vischeck. Available at http://www.vischeck.com /vischeck/, accessed June 13, 2016.
4. Adobe Systems Incorporated. (2016). Adobe Color. Available at http://color .adobe.com, accessed June 13, 2016.
5. Choudhury, A.N.M.I., Potter, K., Rhyne, T-M., et al. (2011). Visualizing Global Correlation in Large-Scale Molecular Biological Data, Biovis 2011 Abstracts. Proceedings of the First IEEE Symposium on Biological Data Visualization, Providence, RI. Available at http://biovis.net/2011/materials /abstracts/BioVispaper120.pdf, accessed June 13, 2016.
6. Scientific Computing and Imaging Institute at the University of Utah. (2016). News from the SCI Institute. Available at http://sci.utah.edu/, accessed June 13, 2016.
7. BroadbandIO. (2016). Who We Are and What We Do. Available at https:// ncbroadband.gov/about-broadbandio/, accessed June 13, 2016.
8. *Triangle Business Journal*. (2011). The e-NC Authority. Available at http:// www.bizjournals.com/triangle/feature/the-e-nc-authority.html, accessed June 13, 2016.
9. ColorBrewer. (2016). ColorBrewer 2.0: Color Advice for Cartography. Available at http://colorbrewer2.org/, accessed June 13, 2016.
10. Pantone. (2016). Studio. Available at https://www.pantone.com/studio, accessed August 4, 2016.
11. Adobe Systems Incorporated. (2016). Adobe Capture CC. Available at http://www.adobe.com/products/capture.html, accessed June 13, 2016.

12. Hill, K.A. and Lackmann, G. (2011). The impact of future climate change on TC intensity and structure: A downscaling approach. *Journal of Climate*, 24: 4644–4661.
13. Renaissance Computing Institute. (2008). The Future Perfect Storm. Available at http://renci.org/news/the-future-perfect-storm/, accessed June 13, 2016.
14. Lawrence Livermore National Laboratory. (2016). VisIt. Available at https://wci.llnl.gov/simulation/computer-codes/visit/, accessed June 13, 2016.
15. Digital Media Interactive LLC. (2012). Color Companion—Analyzer & Converter. Available at https://itunes.apple.com/us/app/color-companion-analyzer-converter/id47794973?mt=8 , accessed June 13, 2016.
16. Paletton.com. (2016). Color Scheme Designer. Available at www.paletton.com, accessed June 13, 2016.
17. Rhyne, T.-M. (2011). Exploring visualization theory. *IEEE Computer Graphics and Applications*, 31: 6–7.

CHAPTER 7

Review of Basic Concepts Covered

I N THIS BOOK, we have highlighted the principles of a body of knowledge called *color theory* and how to apply these concepts to creating digital media and visualization. In this final chapter of our journey, we review some of the highlights of each chapter and note some key issues for future consideration.

7.1 HIGHLIGHTS FROM CHAPTER 1

We began our journey with a description of color models in Chapter 1. We showed that there are three basic color models: (1) the Red, Green, and Blue (RGB) color model for displays; (2) the Cyan, Magenta, Yellow, and Key Black (CMYK) color model for printing; and (3) the Red, Yellow, and Blue (RYB) color model for paints. Next, we provided a brief overview of the historical progression of color theory and reviewed Isaac Newton's creation of the color circle, Moses Harris' pioneering detailed diagram of the RYB color wheel, Johann Wolfgang von Goethe's color wheel of complementary colors, and Michel Chevreul's development of the theory of simultaneous contrasts. We also provided an example of applying Chevreul's theories of color harmony to an Orange and Cyan contrasting color scheme for a treemap visualization. Chevreul was one of the first color theorists to write extensively on the notion that the appearance of a given color changes according to the other hues surrounding it and its resulting context. Figure 7.1 provides a visual summary of highlights from Chapter 1.

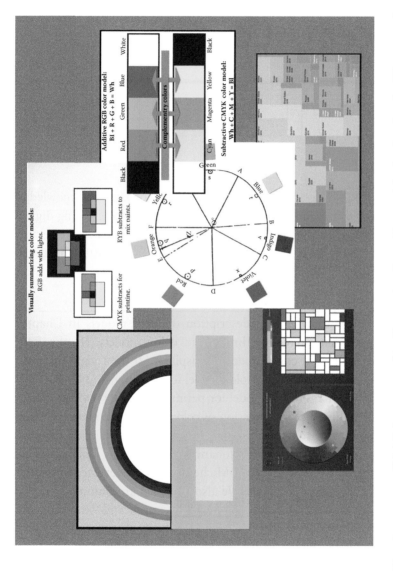

FIGURE 7.1 Visual summary of highlights presented in Chapter 1; refer to Chapter 1 for further details. (Illustration by Theresa-Marie Rhyne, 2016.)

As we noted in Chapter 1, many concepts of color theory evolved based on the RYB color model of painters. At the end of Chapter 1, we referred you to these historic and key references on color theory. Stepping outside of digital media, we refer you to James Gurney's book on *Color and Light: A Guide for the Realist Painter* for a painter's perspective on the application of color. For a photographer's perspective on working with RGB and CMYK color models, we refer you to Jerod Foster's book *Color: A Photographer's Guide to Directing the Eye, Creating Visual Depth, and Conveying Emotion* [1,2].

7.2 HIGHLIGHTS FROM CHAPTER 2

In Chapter 2, we reviewed color vision principles such as trichromatic color vision and opponent color theory that together help explain how our eyes and brain process color information. We began the chapter by highlighting the visible spectrum of light with wavelengths of approximately 390–780 nm and ranging from Violet, Indigo, Blue, Green, Yellow, Orange, and Red. In a reverse order, this is often noted as the ROYGBIV or Roy G. Biv acronym. An overview of human vision fundamentals noted that the key biological components of vision are the eye, the visual center in the brain, and the optic nerve that connects the two. We explored further the Young–Helmholtz theory of trichromatic color vision. This theory asserts that there are three types of cones and each is optimized to absorb a different spectrum range of visible light. One set of cones absorbs long waves of light in the Red range. A second set of cones absorbs middle waves of light in the Green range. The third set of cones absorbs short waves of light in the Blue range. Next, we reviewed Ewald Hering's opponent color theory that challenged trichromatic color vision. Hering proposed that color vision occurred in three channels where opposite colors are in competition and do not mix. These channels are (1) a Red Green channel, (2) a Yellow Blue channel, and (3) a Black and White channel. We showed how color vision researchers, Leo Hurvich and Dorothea Jameson, demonstrated that the theories of Young–Helmholtz and Hering coexisted together. Young and Helmholtz's theory of trichromatic color vision explains what happens with our eyes at the photoreceptor level. Hering's opponent processing color theory explains aspects of color vision processing at the neural level when images are transferred from the eye to the brain via the optic nerve.

We went on to explore how we have three independent channels for conveying color information to our brain or trichromacy. We worked through an example showing that the brain requires at least two of these channels for color vision. We also examined how the brain has no means of distinguishing between a set of single wavelengths and a set of wavelengths combined that produce the same color. This concept of metamerism is used in engineering electronic displays that we use on a daily basis. Colorimetry, the science of color measurement and matching, was introduced as well as luminosity, the perceived brightness of a color.

We continued Chapter 2 with a discussion of color deficiencies or color blindness. We reviewed the following key color deficiencies of Red–Green (protanopia), Green–Red (deuteranopia), and Blue–Yellow (tritanopia). Online tools that provide assistance in showing what images look like to individuals with color deficiencies were reviewed. Additionally, we worked through an example of applying color deficiency studies to a color wheel (or pie chart) that also represents the primary and secondary colors of the RYB color model. These colors on the wheel include Red, Orange, Yellow, Green, Blue, and Purple. Our color deficiency simulation showed how individuals with color deficiencies are unable to easily distinguish between these six colors.

Finally, we discussed how the use of a rainbow color map in visualizing data potentially produces perceptual errors in analyzing trends in the data. This is due to the nonperceptual uniformity of the distances between the Red, Orange, Yellow, Green, Blue, Indigo, and Violet hues in the color spectrum. At the end of Chapter 2, we noted references and further reading associated with these topics. Figure 7.2 provides a visual summary of highlights from Chapter 2.

7.3 HIGHLIGHTS FROM CHAPTER 3

In Chapter 3, we reviewed various color gamut, color spaces, color notation systems, and colorimetry concepts that are used widely in color analysis, design, and reproduction. The chapter provided the terminology to understand online and mobile color apps that allow for digital color selection and capture. We noted that color gamut is defined as the range of colors a device can reproduce and almost every device has a different color gamut. Color images on one device such as your mobile phone will look different when printed from your ink jet printer due to the different range of colors of the respective devices. The devices have different color spaces as well since a mobile phone's color space is defined by the RGB display model and the ink jet printer's color space is defined

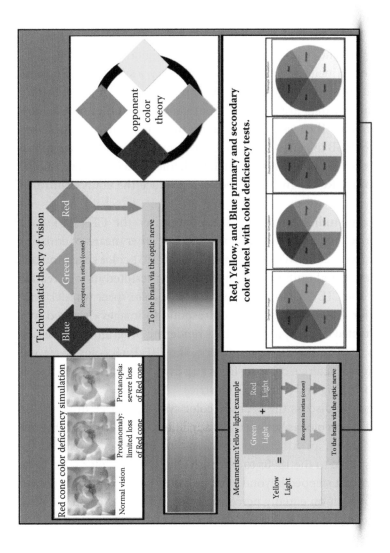

FIGURE 7.2   Visual summary of highlights presented in Chapter 2; refer to Chapter 2 for further details. (Illustration by Theresa-Marie Rhyne, 2016.)

by the CMYK printer's model. We reviewed the commonly applied RGB color spaces of sRGB, Adobe RGB, and ProPhoto RGB. The sRGB color space approximates the color gamut of most RGB display devices. Many software applications and Web specifications are designed around the sRGB specification. Adobe RGB is aimed at providing fewer challenges in transferring from the RGB display devices to the CMYK printing output devices. ProPhoto RGB is designed to offer a color gamut larger than sRGB to support the requirements of high-end digital photography.

Next, we examined the concepts of colorimetry, a system of color measurement based on the concept of equivalent-appearing stimuli to human eyes. Colorimetry data are gathered from empirical studies of matching colors by humans. The task of each human subject is to use the three primary lights of RGB to match a designated *reference* color. When a match is established, the reference color can then be defined in terms of the amount of the respective RGB lights required to reproduce the equivalent reference color.

Colorimetry studies formed the foundation for the CIE 1931 color space, developed to be independent of devices or other means of emission or reproduction of color. We highlighted the CIE 1931 color space and discussed its perceptual uniformity limitations that resulted in the creation of CIE LUV and CIE LAB in 1976. The CIE LUV color space was designed specifically for emissive colors that correspond to images captured by a camera or created by computer graphics rendering programs. As a result, CIE LUV is used in the display industry. The CIE LAB color space was developed to characterize color surfaces and dyes. CIE LAB is used widely in the color imaging and printing industries.

We went on to discuss the Munsell color system, a three-dimensional model that defines color as having three attributes: hue, value, and chroma. Albert H. Munsell, an American artist and art educator, developed the color order system in the 1890s to establish a notation of color with a systematic order that stepped beyond what he called *misleading* color names. The system is built on equally perceived color differences in the shape of branching geometry defined as a color tree. The Munsell color order system has served and continues to serve as the basis for a variety of government and industry specifications.

Next, we examined hue, saturation, and value (HSV) and hue, saturation, and lightness (HSL) color spaces. These three-dimensional cylindrical-coordinate representations of the RGB color model were established to create intuitively easier and more perceptually relevant mixing of additive RGB color lights. Many *color picking* tools on digital devices have been based on these color models. Members of the computer graphics community developed HSV and HSL.

We then highlighted Web colors, noting that the World Wide Web Consortium (W3C) color specifications are based on the sRGB color model. We then covered the HTML–HEX triplet format for color notation. Web colors can be specified in three formats: RGB values, HEX triplet format, or HSL values. We also reviewed Web safe colors and provided an example of Web color selection with the Color Companion mobile app.

The final color space we highlighted was the Pantone color-matching system (PMS), a proprietary color space used primarily in printing and graphic design. Pantone matching methods utilize the Pantone numbering system to identify colors. Individuals located in different geographic locations can refer to particular PMS values to ensure that colors match without making direct personal contact with each other. The Pantone color guides consist of narrow cardboard sheets (approximately 6 × 2 in or 15 × 5 cm) that are printed on one side with rectangular samples showing the different Pantone colors. The guide is bound together at one end to allow for opening the strips out in a fanlike manner. Pantone also provides a mobile PANTONE Studio app for iOS platforms. The app provides a digital display of color swatches for creating a color palette from scratch. The PANTONE Studio app also allows for capturing colors from a digital image or photograph located on or transferred to the app's designated mobile phone. The PANTONE Studio app provides data about sRGB, HTML (HEX triplet), and CMYK values of specified Pantone colors. We worked through examples of the PANTONE Studio app's display of color swatches and color capture features.

It is important to continue to remember a key concept about color gamut: Viewing a color in digital or virtual color spaces does not always mean that the color will appear the same in printed or physical color spaces. This is because of the differences in the RGB color model for display, the CMYK color model for printing, and the RYB color model for painting. Although physical comparison of color specimens to carefully prepared paint chips or color samples can be considered out-of-date with regard to digital media, it turns out to be one of the more accurate methods of color matching. This is because any digital color library cannot depict color specimens consistently or accurately due to the color gamut constraints of RGB display devices. Figure 7.3 provides a visual summary of highlights from Chapter 3.

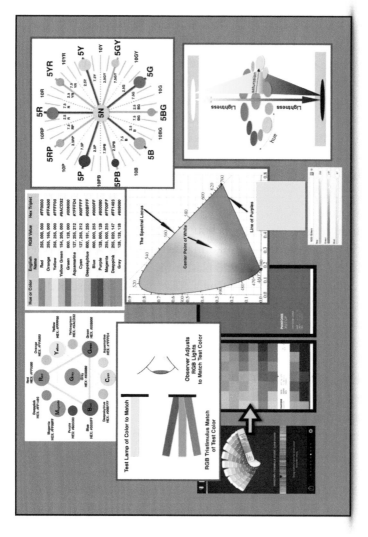

FIGURE 7.3 Visual summary of highlights presented in Chapter 3; refer to Chapter 3 for further details. (Illustration by Theresa-Marie Rhyne, 2016.)

7.4 HIGHLIGHTS FROM CHAPTER 4

In Chapter 4, we defined the language of color harmony based on the color wheel and colorized infographics examples using color harmony principles. We began with a review of the steps for constructing the RGB color wheel for displays, the CMYK color wheel for printing, and the RYB color wheel for painting. We showed how the RGB and CMYK color wheels are inversely related and collapse into one RGB/CMYK color wheel. We defined the primary colors, secondary colors, and tertiary colors for each wheel and diagrammed them as well. We defined the hues, tints, tones, and shades of colors. Hues are the brightest and purest form of colors and reside on the outside of the color wheel. Tints are hues mixed with White and reside on a tint ring next to the hue colors. Tones are hues mixed with Gray and reside on the third tone ring next to the tint ring. Shades are hues mixed with Black and reside on the inner shade ring between the tone ring and the neutral zone of Gray on the color wheel. We then described warm and cool colors on the color wheel.

Next, we defined color harmony as the process of choosing colors, from the color wheel, that work well together in the composition of an image. Nine types of color harmony with an example for each were presented: (1) monochromatic, (2) analogous, (3) complementary, (4) split complementary, (5) analogous complementary, (6) double complementary, (7) tetrad (rectangular and square), (8) diad, and (9) triad. We then reviewed a color wheel or gamut masking approach to defining a specific range of colors or color harmony and showed how to use the *Gamut Mask* tool developed by James Gurney and Richard Robinson.

We revisited the historical evolution of the color wheel and color harmony building on our preliminary review in Section 1.4. In Section 4.7, we provided more details of contributions by Isaac Newton, Moses Harris, Johann Wolfgang von Goethe, and Michel Chevreul. We introduced the Philipp Otto Runge's color sphere contribution and how it initially influenced Albert Munsell's efforts as well as impacted the teachings at the Bauhaus art school. We reviewed the writings of George Field and Ogden N. Rood on chromatics and color harmony that influenced painters, especially impressionists, of their time. Next, the contributions of Louis Prang and Milton Bradley to art education at the elementary and secondary levels, using the RYB color wheel, were noted. We then highlighted teachings of the preliminary course and color concepts at the Bauhaus school, which operated in Germany and combined a unique approach to design with crafts and fine arts. In the Bauhaus discussion, we featured the teaching of color concepts by Paul Klee, Wassily Kandinsky, Johannes Itten, and Josef Albers. We concluded our historical evolution featuring Josef Albers' *Interaction of Color* book from Yale University Press that has now been modernized into a mobile iPad app. Albers' exercises teach, by hands-on application, the concept that the appearance of a color changes according to its context and is greatly influenced by the other hues and lighting surrounding it.

Color harmony concepts have been applied to many disciplines. In our discussion of the historical evolutions of the color wheel, we highlighted a few individual contributions oriented toward the Western world. As you explore color theory further, you may find inspiration from other contributors and disciplines. Reference [3] provides a discussion of the color theory from the interior design and architecture perspective. Figure 7.4 provides a visual summary of highlights from Chapter 4.

7.5 HIGHLIGHTS FROM CHAPTER 5

In Chapter 5, we examined eight tools for analyzing and creating color palettes (1) Adobe Color CC, (2) Adobe Capture CC, (3) the COLOURlovers community and its Color Palette Software (COPASO) tool, (4) Paletton's Color Scheme Designer, (5) Color Companion, (6) PANTONE Studio, (7) ColorBrewer 2.0, and (8) the *Interaction of Color by Josef Albers* iPad app. We discussed key features of each tool and showed how each respective tool can be used to analyze or create a color palette. Adobe Color CC, the COLOURlovers community, Paletton's Color Scheme Designer, and ColorBrewer 2.0 are online resources. Adobe Capture CC, Color Companion, PANTONE Studio, and the *Interaction of Color by Josef Albers* iPad app are mobile apps. Adobe Color CC, Adobe Capture CC, the COLOURlovers' COPASO tool, Paletton's Color Scheme Designer, Color Companion, and PANTONE Studio include concepts of color harmony in their respective color palette applications. We discussed the language of color harmony in Chapter 4.

Adobe Capture CC is specifically targeted at building color palettes from a captured or stored image on your mobile device. The Color Companion and PANTONE Studio apps provide similar functionality. Adobe Color CC and COLOURlovers' COPASO also support importing an image into their respective tools for color analyses. Color Companion

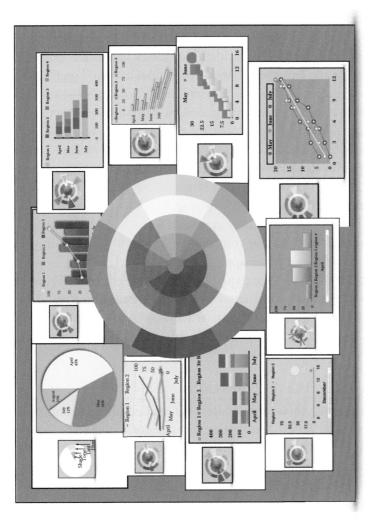

FIGURE 7.4 Visual summary of highlights presented in Chapter 4; refer to Chapter 4 for further details. (Illustration by Theresa-Marie Rhyne, 2016.)

provides a color mixing function that can be used to explore novel RGB and RYB color combinations. Paletton's Color Scheme Designer specifically states that it applies the fundamentals of artistic color theory and provides examples for designing Web sites with the RYB color model. The PANTONE Studio app is focused on providing color solutions in regard to the proprietary Pantone color matching system (PMS). However, the PANTONE Studio app provides information about the corresponding RGB, Web HEX, and CMYK values associated with the recommended PMS solutions. ColorBrewer 2.0 provides color advice specifically oriented toward geographic and data visualization and defines its own classification system for these purposes. However, we have shown how ColorBrewer can be used for other color scheme design purposes. Although the *Interaction of Color by Josef Albers* iPad app is focused on serving as a teaching tool, we showed how color scheme solutions often result from working with the respective template examples. Paletton's Color Scheme Designer and ColorBrewer 2.0 provide methods for addressing color blindness or color deficiency concerns directly in their online applications.

Each tool has its own particular approach for aiding, creating, and assessing color schemes. As you continue on in your color studies, you will likely find additional color applications that work as part of your own digital color toolbox. One paper application worth considering is a pocket or larger color wheel from *The Color Wheel Company*. This pocket color wheel is 5.125 in in diameter while a larger size is 9.25 in in diameter [4]. Figure 7.5 provides a visual summary of highlights from Chapter 5.

7.6 HIGHLIGHTS FROM CHAPTER 6

Chapter 6 highlighted three case studies that applied principles of color theory to data visualization. The first project discussed how color theory concepts were applied to the visualization of correlation in large-scale molecular biological data. The Munsell color order system provided inspiration for the layout of the visual data while the Vischeck tool assisted in examining color deficiencies associated with various suggested color harmonies for the visualization matrix. The selected complementary color harmony was verified with the Adobe Color tool before the final biological visualization was completed.

The second project described the development of a household broadband availability map of the state of North Carolina. ColorBrewer was used to establish the initial color scheme while the PANTONE Studio app

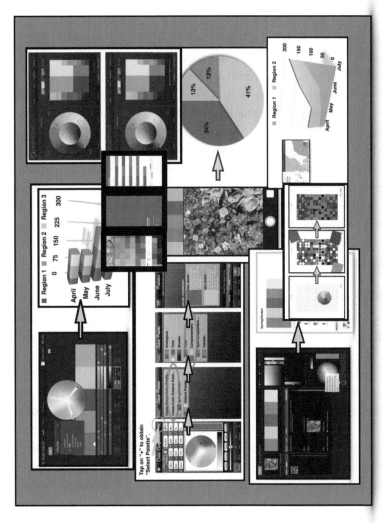

FIGURE 7.5 Visual summary of highlights presented in Chapter 5; refer to Chapter 5 for further details. (Illustration by Theresa-Marie Rhyne, 2016.)

provided color recommendations for printed versions of the map. The final color scheme was verified with the Adobe Capture app.

The third project applied Michel Chevreul's principles of color harmony and color contrasts to depicting the times series animation for a computationally modeled tropical storm. ColorBrewer was again used to establish the overall color scheme. It was also shown how the Color Companion app could be used to create individual colormaps for data variables in the VisIt visualization and animation tool. Paletton's online Color Scheme Designer tool was used to depict the analogous Blue, Purple, and Magenta color harmony of the resulting rain water isosurfaces and *GLW* cloud cover as well as the complementary Orange and Blue Green color harmony of the wind vectors against the ocean–land mass mask.

These three examples demonstrated how several of the color tools noted in Chapter 5 could be combined together for color analyses, including color deficiency assessments. The fundamentals of color harmony and contrasts are also incorporated into these tools. At the end of Chapter 6, we provided references regarding how to find out more details about the given case study described. Figure 7.6 provides a visual summary of highlights from Chapter 6.

7.7 CONCLUDING REMARKS

In this book, we have provided an overview of the fundamentals of color theory and terminology associated with color science. We defined the language of color harmony based on the color wheel. Additionally, some historical perspective on the evolution of the color theory, from the Western world viewpoint, was provided. Next, we showed how this language is incorporated into online and mobile color apps that allow for digital color selection and capture. Although we have shown several approaches to color scheme development, the creation of a specific color palette is targeted at the needs and requirements of the particular project that is under way. Our suggestions are color advice with the final solutions being your choices of color selection for your unique tasks and objectives. We have only begun to introduce the fundamental concepts of color theory as applied to digital media and visualization in this book. We hope you continue to have your own discoveries exploring the world of color that surrounds us.

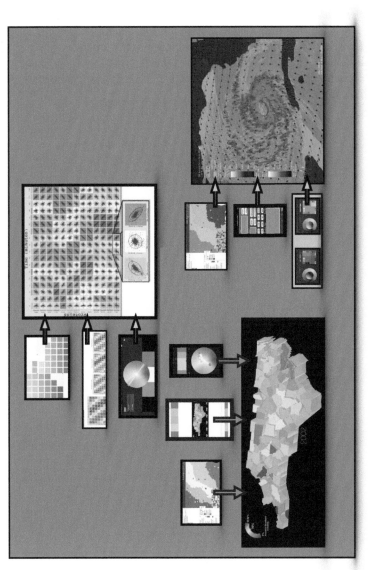

FIGURE 7.6 Visual summary of highlights presented in Chapter 6; refer to Chapter 6 for further details. (Illustration by Theresa-Marie Rhyne, 2016.)

REFERENCES

1. Gurney, J. (2010). *Color and Light: A Guide for the Realist Painter.* Kansas City, MO: Andrews McMeel Publishing.
2. Foster, J. (2014). *Color: A Photographer's Guide to Directing the Eye, Creating Visual Depth and Conveying Emotion.* San Francisco, CA: Peachpit Press.
3. Sickler, D. (2010). *The Keys to Color: A Decorator's Handbook for Coloring Paints, Plasters and Glazes.* Seattle, WA: Createspace.
4. The Color Wheel Company. (2016). Color Wheels. Available at http://color-wheelco.com/buy-now/#!/Color-Wheels/c/13375266/offset=0&sort=normal, accessed June 14, 2016.

Index

Printed and bound by CPI Group (UK) Ltd, Croydon, CR0 4YY

21/10/2024

01777108-0005